THE WAY OF
HARMONY

*A Guide to Self-Knowledge Through
the Arts of T'ai Chi Chuan, Hsing I,
Pa Kua, and Chi Kung*

By Howard Reid

with Danny Connor, Lam Kam Chuen,
Nigel Sutton and Robin Rusher

Photography by Fausto Dorelli

A GAIA ORIGINAL

A FIRESIDE BOOK
PUBLISHED BY SIMON & SCHUSTER INC
NEW YORK LONDON TORONTO SYDNEY TOKYO

A GAIA ORIGINAL

Written by Howard Reid

with Danny Connor
    Lam Kam Chuen
    Nigel Sutton
    Robin Rusher

Photography by Fausto Dorelli

Editorial	Roslin Mair
Design	Sara Mathews
Illustration	Debbie Hinks
	Brian McKenzie
Calligraphy	Mew Hong Tan
Production	Susan Walby
Direction	Lucy Lidell
	Casey Horton, Patrick Nugent

Simon and Schuster/Fireside Books,
Published by Simon & Schuster Inc.
Simon & Schuster Building
Rockefeller Center
1230 Avenue of the Americas
New York, New York 10020

SIMON AND SCHUSTER, FIRESIDE, and
colophons are registered trademarks of Simon &
Schuster Inc.

First published in 1988 in Great Britain
by Unwin Hyman Limited, London

Library of Congress Cataloging in Publication Data

Reid, Howard.
    The way of harmony: a guide to self-knowledge through the arts of
T'ai Chi Chuan, Hsing I, Pa Kua, and Chi Kung / by Howard Reid:
with Danny Connor ... [et al.] ; photography by Fausto Dorelli.
          p.   cm.
    "A Gaia original."
    Includes index.
    ISBN 0-671-67010-7.   ISBN 0-671-66632-0 (A Fireside book : pbk.)
    1. Exercise.   2. Exercise therapy.   3. Medicine, Chinese.
    I. Title.
RA781.R35 1989   88-16946
613.7--dc19   CIP

10 9 8 7 6 5 4 3 2 1
10 9 8 7 6 5 4 3 2 1 Pbk.

Printed and bound in Spain by
Artes Graficas Toledo S.A.
D.L.TO.: 895-1988 Pbk

Notes on pronunciation of Chinese terms

The key words in this book are sets of Chinese characters
representing concepts rather than sounds. While the written
language of China, Standard Chinese or Mandarin, is common
to hundreds of millions of Chinese nationals, the spoken word
is far more complicated. There is a bewildering array of
regional and local dialects – a Cantonese cannot understand
spoken Mandarin at all, and someone from Shanghai is barely
intelligible to either of the latter. This situation inevitably
complicates attempts to give standard Chinese pronunciation
for Westerners. There are, however, traditional Western
pronunciations for the chief terms used in this book:

> **Chi** is pronounced "chee"; **Tan Tien** "dan dee-en";
> **Chi Kung** "chee goong"; **Ba Duan Jin** "ba doo-wan
> jin"; **Hsing I** is "sing yee", with a slight aspiration on
> the "s"; **Pa Kua** is "ba gwa"; and **T'ai Chi Chuan** is
> pronounced "tie chee choo-wan".

Unfortunately, this standard usage has a few inconsistencies.
Ba and pa are both pronounced "ba" (both mean eight); and
Hsing I and Pa Kua should be fully titled as Hsing I Chuan
and Pa Kua Chang.

Spellings of Chinese terms

The spellings used in this edition are also standard in Western
martial arts' usage. However, it should be noted that the Pin
Yin transliteration advised by the People's Republic of China,
and thought by some to give a closer indication of correct
pronunciation, is now predominant in the Western media (for
example, Peking is spelled *Beijing*). The Pin Yin spellings of
the key Chinese words used in this book are as follows:

> **Chi** – *Qi*; **Tan tien** – *Dan tien*; **Chi Kung** – *Qi Gong*;
> **Ba Duan Jin** – *Ba Duan Gin*; **Hsing I** – *Xing Yi*; **Pa Kua**
> – *Ba Gua*; **T'ai Chi Chuan** – *Tai Ji Quan*.

Special martial arts' terms

There are other special martial terms apart from the Chinese
words mentioned above. Most common of these is the verb
"to circle", which applies to arm movements within the
exercises. Whether you are circling up or down, or to one side
or the other, this action is a smooth, rounded one, with the
movement of the curved arm describing an arc. The arrows
that appear in the illustrations of the exercises will help to
guide you in the circling movements. Another word
commonly used in the martial arts is "form", meaning an
exercise or position. A form may be an extended sequence,
such as the T'ai Chi Short Form, or just a few steps, as in the
Twelve Animal forms in Hsing I.

Contents

Introduction   8

PART ONE   *The Soft Arts*   21

1: Chi Kung *Breath power*   22

2: Hsing I *Ways to harmony*   44

3: Pa Kua *Eternal change*   64

4: T'ai Chi Chuan *The art of awareness*   82

PART TWO   *The Balanced Way*   147

5: Oriental paths to balance   148

6: Therapeutic uses   172

Index and bibliography   189

All things are backed by the Shade (Yin)
And faced by the light (Yang),
And harmonized by the immaterial Breath (Chi).

From Lao Tzu's *Tao Te Ching*

Introduction

To many people, the martial arts conjure up visions of an Oriental combatant flying through the air or a pile of bricks being shattered by a karate chop. The images are of aggression, violence and destruction. Yet to see the martial arts in this light is to ignore their philosophical content and to overlook a very important branch of the arts. For within this family of Chinese movement forms there is in fact a series – the "soft" or "internal" arts – that has developed way beyond the narrow confines of combat skills. Comprising Chi Kung, T'ai Chi Chuan, Hsing I, and Pa Kua, the soft arts have reached such levels of refinement that they are designed to create within their practitioners a deep sense of the unity of body, mind and soul, and are actually used to heal injury and cure sickness. These arts have evolved into methods of personal development, which are unique and unsurpassed, and they bring a deep sense of the richness and unity of life to those who study them.

But why should you want to try one of the soft martial arts? One of the most compelling reasons for learning the soft arts is that they provide a complete and systematic programme of exercise which will invigorate your entire body, with minimal risk of strain or injury. All the exercises contained in this book are safe for people of all ages to use, and they reach almost every part of your body. In fact, the Chinese believe that doing these exercises actually massages and invigorates internal organs like your heart and liver, as well as your muscles, tendons, and joints. Sports like tennis, squash, or running, by contrast, only exercise some parts of your body, and it is comparatively easy to strain a muscle if you over-exert yourself.

More important, though, the soft arts lead you to new levels of self-knowledge and awareness, and teach you how your body relates to your mind and to your inner being, your soul. Training in these arts will help you to discover and develop the inner, deeper side of yourself – a side that so many of us tend to ignore or hide away. Like Yoga, the soft arts are built upon the foundations of ancient Oriental philosophy. They are forms of moving meditation. But they differ from Yoga in one vital way – even the most refined forms, like T'ai Chi

Soft martial duets
Only one of the soft arts taught in Part One of this book includes exercises where you need a partner. In T'ai Chi Chuan, both the Basic Powers and Pushing Hands (pp.140-6) are team exercises that were devised to develop your sense of balance and your self-defence capabilities.

Chuan, still contain a self-defence component. In physical terms, this may or may not be important to you, but it is vital mentally and emotionally. Only Chi Kung, Chapter 1, is without this obvious martial aspect.

This book is for those who want to combine the physical skills of the martial arts with a deeper mental approach. While Part One will guide you through each art in turn, Part Two will help to complement the technical skills you have learned by offering you a new, more balanced approach to life as a whole.

The soft arts versus the hard

How then do these soft or internal arts differ from their better-known cousins – the "hard" or "external" arts like Karate, Kung Fu or Tae Kwon Do? The differences are partly technical. Hard arts like Karate use very vigorous training programmes, and teach the students both offensive and defensive techniques. Kicks, punches, chops, and stabs are taught alongside blocks and evasive techniques. These arts are called "hard" because they basically oppose force with force. They are called "external" because the force is for the most part created by exerting muscle power, mainly from the outer limbs – the legs and arms. Arts like T'ai Chi Chuan are called "soft" because they use evasions, throws, leverage, and pushes, rather than force to overcome an attacker. They are generally defensive rather than offensive, using an aggressor's own force to subdue him or her with the absolute minimum of effort. The soft arts are also known as internal arts because they train you to use intelligence to overcome an aggressor.

But the main difference between the two classes of art lies in their mental approach to the challenge of staying alive, fit, and healthy in an uncertain world. Although there is a lot of overlap in their theoretical content, exponents of the hard arts tend to stress the need for an intuitive physical response – that is, without thought or mind – to a threatening situation, while soft artists always aim for the ascendancy of the mind over the body. The soft arts have therefore generally developed more profound schools of thought and action, focusing on the Chinese understanding of nature and the

Oriental workouts
Millions of people in the Far East – in the People's Republic of China, Singapore, Malaysia, Hong Kong, Japan, and Korea – use the beautiful dance-like forms of T'ai Chi Chuan as a daily exercise, practising outside in the fresh air, developing and regulating the Chi or vital energy.

Universe. Training in these arts teaches the student to react naturally and calmly in stressful situations, and not to be confused by technique, fear or uncertainty. A skilled soft artist understands that the will or mind commands, strength obeys, and energy follows.

Origins and philosophies of the arts

It is likely that the martial arts in the broadest sense are as old as humanity itself. Various artefacts, sculptures and engravings from ancient Sumeria and Babylon depict wrestling and ritualized combat, and scenes on the walls of many pharoahs' tombs show warriors in similar poses. Some of these items are 5,000 years old. But the dates are really irrelevant, for ritualized fighting must certainly predate existing records. The point is that such behaviour is part of human nature.

Nobody knows at what point people began to refine battlefield arts into the ancient antecedents of today's martial arts, but the clues to the origins of the arts lie in the history of India and the Far East between 2,500 and 1,500 years ago. Curiously, these clues centre around the development of religion and philosophy rather than around politics or technology.

The period from 500 BC to the birth of Christ was an extraordinarily rich era for people in both the West and the East. In the West, classical Greek civilization flourished, and in the East the great philosophies of Taoism, Confucianism, and Buddhism were all born. These systems remain the pillars of Asian thought today, even within the People's Republic of China.

Taoism was formalized by the sage Lao Tzu and his successors between 600 and 300 BC, but it is based on even more ancient beliefs. At the heart of Taoism lies the conviction that human beings are part of nature, and that the key to understanding ourselves and the world we live in is through increasing our understanding of nature. Tao, the Way, is that single force which gives being, form, sense, and energy to all things. The best way to understand Tao and hence ourselves is through the study of the natural world. You will see how central this idea is to the soft arts in Hsing I, Chapter 2, in the Five Element exercises, and the Twelve Animals.

The essence of Taoism lies in the *Tao Te Ching* – perhaps China's greatest literary masterpiece. Traditionally ascribed to Lao Tzu, the style of the *Tao Te Ching* suggests a date of about 300 BC. Within its few pages and phrases rest the kernels of Taoist thought, presented in a highly mystical manner. However, its relevance to all soft martial arts should never be underestimated.

Historically, it is known that by about the time of Christ, physicians in China had absorbed the Taoist views expressed in the *Tao Te Ching* into some of their practices, and that they had evolved a series of remedial exercises, which entailed mimicking the movements of animals like the horse, tiger, or dragon. At what point this approach was applied specifically to the fighting behaviour of these animals we simply do not know. But it seems clear that it is here that the origins of the movements of the soft arts lie.

Along with the *Tao Te Ching*, perhaps the most important ancient Chinese text is the *I Ching*, the Book of Changes, whose origins go back almost 3,000 years. It is believed to have been written in part by Confucius, and certainly deeply influenced his thought. At its heart the Book of Changes extends the Taoist view of nature through time. Its central argument is that reality is fundamentally fluid, a constant flow of events through which we pass in life. All attempts to create permanence and fixity are illusions, and obstruct our path to the truly transient state that is the basic reality. The nature of the Tao, then, is constant and incessant change. Although, once again, there is no clear evidence of the time and place when this emphasis on constant change became integrated into the practice of the soft martial arts, the philosophy of change lies at the heart of all of them – and it is particularly relevant to the practice of Pa Kua.

At the same time that Taoism and Confucianism were growing up in China, so Buddhism was born and spread, first in India, then through South-east Asia, and eventually to China. From about the time of Christ, monks, scholars, and diplomats began to travel the Silk Road between the great civilizations of China and India, and Buddhism took root in parts of China. With its emphasis on meditation, asceticism, and spiritual attainment, it was quickly adopted in China, and partly absorbed into the other Chinese philosophies. The precise point when Buddhism began to intermingle with the other elements that compose the soft martial arts is uncertain. It seems hard now to imagine the arts without the wisdom of the ancient Buddhist sages. One of these characters has come down to us through the centuries, albeit in semi-mythical form.

It is said that around 520 AD a tall, blue-eyed Indian (or possibly Persian) Buddhist monk travelled the Silk Road until he came to the beautiful Songshan Shaolin Temple in Central China. His name was Bodhidharma in India, Ta Mo in China. There he spent many years facing a wall, "listening to the ants scream" (or seeking enlightenment). Having attained enlightenment, he founded the famous Ch'an or Zen school of Buddhism. At the temple he is said to have taught the monks self-defence, to aid them in their mendicant wanderings and as a path to enlightenment. Though today he is mainly recognized as the founder of the external forms of the arts, Bodhidharma is revered by all martial artists as the one who introduced Wu Te – the "martial virtues" of discipline, restraint, humility and respect for human life – to the martial arts. He taught that the arts should be used only to promote health and spiritual development, not for fighting. In this sense, then, he formulated the mental approach to physical training which still guides all soft martial artists.

The fusion of these three great strands of Eastern thought forms the foundations of the soft martial arts as they are practised today. The sages who founded them sought and found ways of transforming the intangible powers of thought and ideas into concrete forms of action, into a series of exercises which allow us to transform mental activity of the highest order into bodily movement. In this way, then, thought becomes action combined with meaning.

The characteristics of the soft arts

In action, the four soft arts look very different, but they have all evolved from a common stock of postures and

Lao Tzu
The philosopher and ascetic Lao Tzu is said to have left the Chinese court and travelled westward, nobody knows where, riding on the back of an ox. Asked at the border to leave something in writing, he wrote the *Tao Te Ching* (see p.13), a small volume that provides the earliest formulation of the Taoist thought underlying the soft martial arts.

movements. Deeply rooted in Eastern culture, they are all devoted to developing and balancing your inner energy (called Chi – or Qi, the new revisionist spelling – by the Chinese), in order to gain greater control over your destiny, and to achieve a happier, better balanced life. Practised regularly, each of the arts can bring you ultimately to a deeper awareness of yourself, and your place in the order of things. So how can you choose which one might be best for you?

Chi Kung is a series of exercises which are mostly static or involve only very slow movement. It contains no fast or jerky movements, so it can be practised by anyone, regardless of age. Its aim is to improve the flow of vital energy – Chi – through your body, and to help you to develop powers of concentration. Chi Kung as it is known today was mainly formalized in the 20th century, but its origins may well lie in the early Chinese therapeutic exercises known as Daoyin, which date back to 700 BC. Most people practise Chi Kung as well as another soft art, but it is in itself a complete art form which can be learned on its own and practised for a lifetime. As a complement to Chi Kung this chapter also shows how to do the Ba Duan Jin – a set of ancient exercises designed to ensure inner and outer health and fitness without strain or over-exertion.

Hsing I is a fast, lively art. Its exercises are athletic and energetic, but they also contain within them principles which are essential to grasping the essence of the soft arts. In common with Chi Kung, Hsing I may also have its origins in the Daoyin – for, like Hsing I, Daoyin used exercises which imitated the movements of animals. The first recorded user of the modern style of Hsing I was Chi Lung-feng from Shanghai, who claims to have learned it from a Taoist in the mid-17th century.

Pa Kua is also an art of speed and power. But it can be performed with hypnotic grace and effortless skill by people aged fifty and over. Tung Hai Chuan (1798-1879) was the first recorded master of Pa Kua. He is said to have been taught it by another Taoist in the mountains of Kiangsu province. The message of Pa Kua is perhaps more profound than all the other soft martial arts: form is captivity, and the loss of form is freedom.

T'ai Chi Chuan is a slow, graceful, dance-like form of movement. It looks easy to do, yet when you first start practising it you find that it calls upon muscles, energy, balance and control that you thought you had but which simply aren't there. Practising it gradually builds up these powers in your body and your mind, creating a wholeness that you never knew you lacked. Clinical trials in China have confirmed that it is specially good for older people, but people of all ages and from all walks of life can benefit from its hauntingly beautiful exercises.

The earliest records of the practice of T'ai Chi date back about 300 years, but it was not formally named until the end of the 18th century, by one Wang Zong Yue. It was brought to Beijing in 1852, from where it spread rapidly throughout China. In the last 100 years many of the faster moves have been taken out, leaving the soft flowing art as we know it today. Traditionally, there are several schools of T'ai Chi in China – the Chen style is the oldest, and the Yang style, formulated in the mid-19th century, is the most popular. But in reality all the schools are very similar. Much more variable is the quality of T'ai Chi instructors, especially outside China.

These then are the characteristics of the family of the soft arts. You may choose to try one, two or all of them. Chi Kung, for example, is often practised together with one of the other more dramatic arts, which, according to some masters, form a series that increases in complexity from Hsing I, to Pa Kua and T'ai Chi Chuan. Each art has its own richness and depth, and each will change you in ways you did not expect. The best way to find out which one will suit you is to try some of the easier exercises in this book – such as the Ba Duan Jin in Chapter 1 – that will warm and gently stretch your body. Then set to work in earnest on the art that feels right for you. Remember, the more you give the soft arts, the more they will repay you.

Getting started

The aim of the soft martial arts is not just to train your body, but to give you mental and spiritual strength through physical movement. By practising these arts you can rediscover your natural self, and learn to move, breathe, and feel as you did in that purest of states when you were newly born. But in order to experience these achievements, it's necessary for you to prepare yourself thoroughly for training, both physically and mentally.

All the internal arts can be performed in normal work clothes, as long as they are not too tight-fitting. But you will probably find it better to put on other clothes, as it helps to change your mood and aids that sense of preparing for something a bit different. In general, people wear track suits or loose-fitting white or black cotton trousers, with a sweatshirt or loose cotton jacket, depending on the temperature of the room used for training. Most martial arts' students in the West prefer to train barefoot, though few do so in China. Training shoes or Chinese Kung Fu slippers are the best footwear, especially if you are exercising outside.

You don't need a training hall to perform the soft arts. Like the millions of Chinese who do them every day, you can practise them in the park or in your garden, or indoors in an uncluttered room. All you need is a flat area, free of obstruction, and about 15 feet (5 m) square. But if the weather is fine, it's good to practise outside in the fresh air, especially under the shade of trees.

Try to exercise at times of the day when you feel fully awake or alert. Most Chinese people train in the early morning, before breakfast, then eat breakfast together. Others prefer to unwind after the day's work by practising in the evening. Many people like to do a few minutes of static meditation before they start to train, to adopt a calm and receptive state of mind. Alternatively, you can try taking a short walk or spend a little while sitting, standing, or lying down quietly. Always take a little time to separate your daily life from training. As you progress in the arts this period of separation may naturally reduce itself to a few moments; ideally, in the end, it will disappear altogether.

If you want to take the soft arts seriously, you should look for a good instructor – but this is easier said than done. For though there are many competent instructors in these arts practising outside China, there are also a large number of instructors with dubious qualifications and inflated pretensions. It is important to find a

Positions from the four soft arts
(From the top, left to right) Position b from Intermediate exercise 3 in Chi Kung (p.40); the Horse, one of the Twelve Animals in Hsing I (p.60); position 8 from the Eight Fixed Postures in Pa Kua (p.74); and a transitional move from Step 9, the Single Whip (pp.110-11), in the T'ai Chi Short Form.

氣功

形意拳

八卦掌

太極拳

qualified teacher, and one who understands the
philosophy of the martial arts, and is therefore able to set
the arts in their broader context. Above all, beware of
those who offer quick paths to enlightenment or cures
for cancer and those who claim knowledge of divine
truths. There are few true gurus, and those who do exist
distinguish themselves, not by exalted self-propaganda,
but by their modesty and humility.

Integrating the soft arts in your life

In order to both achieve and sustain a deeper sense of
balance and harmony, you need to extend the wisdom of
the philosophy behind the soft arts into other aspects of
your life. In Chapter 5, Oriental paths to balance, we
look at how you can identify and correct imbalance in all
the basic areas of your lifestyle – in your eating habits,
your emotional life and sexuality, and in your quest for
spiritual harmony.

The final chapter explains how you can use the
exercises of the soft arts to help yourself – or your family
or friends – to recover from many common ailments and
to ease particular stages of life, such as pregnancy or old
age. Few people in the West realize that the correct type
of exercise can play a major role in treating problems like
anxiety or sleeplessness, as well as aiding more obvious
physical problems like rheumatism and backache.

Incorporating the Taoist wisdom of the Way of
Harmony into your life will not only improve your
physical and mental health, it can also lead you to higher
planes of understanding and awareness. But though this
book can set you on the road, it is ultimately up to you
to put its teachings into practice. Finding the Way is a
constant, never-ending quest that requires a continual
reappraisal of every step you take, every move you
make, and every thought you create.

PART ONE

The Soft Arts

氣功

1: Chi Kung

Breath power

Chi Kung is the simplest but by no means the most superficial of the soft or internal martial arts. Though it is concerned far less with martial ability than the other arts, it is through moulding the body's energy in Chi Kung that the strength to practise all the other arts emerges. Chi Kung literally means "energy work". In common with the other soft arts it has a central principle or goal – that is, the cultivation of Chi, the vital energy. Chi has many meanings – it is energy, it is the life force, but it is also air and breath and even nourishment. It is the fundamental force in the Universe which the martial arts teach you to sense and then to generate, so as to harmonize its flow (see also p.24).

Although each of the soft martial arts is a complete and unified system in its own right, people in China tend to practise them jointly, or to progress from one art to the next (see p.17). Most commonly, students begin with a combination of Chi Kung and T'ai Chi Chuan. As a starting point for training, Chi Kung aims to instil deep natural breathing, and to focus and balance the mind. Included in this chapter is Ba Duan Jin (pp.26-33), a sequence of eight exercises that is often practised with Chi Kung.

All the exercises taught here are wonderfully simple – but perfecting them can be a life's work. Chi Kung is mastered above all by constant practice. Most teachers of the other arts also practise and perfect Chi Kung, but there are many masters who practise Chi Kung alone. Chinese masters of Chi Kung can perform extraordinary feats of strength and endurance by developing the use of Chi, the life force, and concentrating it in specific parts of their bodies. But building up those powers can take years of dedicated training.

Chi Kung is the most fundamental of the martial arts. Diligent practice every day will keep you in good physical and mental shape and promote vitality, and the exercises can be used at any stage in life – in childhood, in adulthood, in pregnancy, and in later life. The belief in the benefits of cultivating your Chi, or vital energy, goes back nearly 3,000 years in Chinese history. One of the classics of ancient Chinese literature, the *Nei Ching*, or Yellow Emperor's Classic of Internal Medicine, records the idea that Chi may be developed through breath control. The Chinese have been practising various exercises similar to Chi Kung ever since, using them to maintain health and to restore it after illness, as well as to strengthen themselves for martial arts' practice. As Chapter 6 shows (pp.172-88), Chi Kung can also be practised to alleviate many types of illness and pain and, since the basic movements are very gentle, many people who suffer from chronic debilitating conditions can embark on a course of therapeutic discipline without risk of injury or strain.

Chi

The sage Lao Tzu, who lived over 2,000 years ago, founded the philosophy known as Taoism that underlies the soft martial arts (see p.12). The Tao is the natural law or Way of the Universe, and at its base lies the following progression: all things are backed by the Shade (Yin) and faced by the Light (Yang), and harmonized by the "immaterial breath", or Chi.

While Tao is "all", Yin and Yang are the fundamental and complementary shades of the Universe. But all things would be static and lifeless without Chi. Chi is the driving force of the cosmos and the driving force of human life, the energy that spurs us on to grow and develop as we pass through life. Without it we would all regress and decay. One of the basic aims of all the soft martial arts is to teach the student how to feel this energy, then to harmonize its flow through the body, and finally to nourish and develop it.

The Chinese believe that Chi exists not only within the cosmos but also within the body, where it courses through our bodies along its own channels called meridians (p.152). Further, they believe that Chi has a centre or home in the lower abdomen (right), a place of concentration where it is stored and where it can be absorbed into the body, the Tan Tien. (Certain gestures in the soft arts' exercises are intended to settle Chi at the Tan Tien.) A blockage or interruption of the flow of Chi can cause sickness, both mental and physical, and one of the first principles of the soft arts is to prevent such blockages, and to help the Chi to flow freely. The way that they achieve this is through natural deep breathing, through relaxed but controlled exercise, and through sustained concentration. Many of the positions in the arts are designed to affect the movement of energy, and to help it to travel around your body and to nourish you internally and externally.

The Ba Duan Jin and Chi Kung exercises taught on pages 26-43 will help you to develop your awareness of Chi, improve your fitness in general, and bring better balance to your body and mind. Practising other soft martial arts will further develop your sensitivity, as will the meditation and special breathing exercises taught in Chapter 5 (pp.166-9).

The Tan Tien
According to the Chinese, Chi has a centre or storehouse in the body known as the Tan Tien, located about 2 inches (5 cm) below the navel. If you are breathing correctly (see facing page) you can feel the Tan Tien moving with your breath. This area is also your body's centre of gravity. For every arm or leg movement you make, however slight, there is a natural counter-balancing movement, and this is always felt at the Tan Tien. Hence it is said that all movement originates at the Tan Tien.

Natural breathing

One of the central aims of the soft martial arts is to train you to breathe correctly. Your breathing should be completely relaxed and natural, with the breath coming from the pit of the stomach, the Tan Tien. Only when your stance is correct and your belly relaxed can your Chi begin to flow properly. This may sound simple, but for many people it requires great concentration – and sustained deliberate breathing is indeed itself a form of meditation. The great Chinese classic, the *Tao Te Ching* asks us: *"Can you keep the soul always concentrated from straying? Can you regulate the breath and become soft and pliant like an infant?"* This state can be achieved, but adults have to concentrate on regulating their breathing for a long time before it comes easily and naturally. Practising the exercise below, by itself, and before your Chi Kung practice, will help you to adjust to the new pattern.

Deep breathing
(This exercise is also known as Yang breathing, see p.167.) Your mouth should be closed, and all your muscles relaxed, the breath moving downward with your diaphragm instead of outward with your chest, the belly protruding to its natural extent while the lungs fill with air. It helps if you focus on the Tan Tien (see facing page), placing your hands on the spot, so that you can feel your belly filling with air and then emptying. Many Westerners find this posture hard to adopt, but it is essential in the martial arts.

In *Inhale deeply through your nose, letting your belly fill naturally. Breathe slowly and deeply, but without noise or needless effort.*

Out *Exhale through your nose from the Tan Tien, until you feel naturally empty of air. Continue this deep breathing for about 5 minutes. As your concentration develops you should begin to feel the vital energy travelling through the nose to the lungs and to the Tan Tien, then up and out again.*

Ba Duan Jin

This set of eight exercises (the Eight Fine Exercises, in translation) is often practised with Chi Kung. The movements provide a comprehensive system of exercise for people of all ages, toning up muscles and stimulating the flow of Chi throughout the body. You should perform them quite vigorously if you are in good health, to help build up your strength and suppleness, but if you are ill or in your later years you should practise more gently. In all cases, try to move smoothly, and imagine the action described in the subtitle, for example, that you are touching the sky in Exercise 1. (The subtitles also describe the effect of your actions on your body.) Each exercise is performed eight times, and the stretched position is held for 1 second. They are all practised facing to the front (though for clarity, some are illustrated from different angles).

Starting position
Stand with your feet about shoulders' width apart. Let your hands rest naturally by your sides, and grip the ground lightly with your toes. Look straight ahead.

Exercise 1
Regulate the Internal Organs by Raising Both Hands to the Sky

You should exhale as your arms move outward and inhale as they move inward. Keep your breathing slow, deep, and relaxed.

1a *Raise your arms slowly and smoothly until your hands are in front of your chest, the palms of your hands facing inward. Remember to exhale on the outward movement.*

1a

1b *Continue lifting your arms, turning the palms of the hands outward as they pass your face. As your hands move above your head the palms should be facing upward, the fingers pointing toward each other.*

1b

1c *Push both hands up toward the sky, palms upward, arms as straight as you can make them. At the same time push into the ground with your feet, stretching your whole body from top to toe. Hold the position for 1 second, then relax and inhale. If you are new to Ba Duan Jin, complete the exercise here.*

1c

1d *When you have trained for some time, continue upward from 1c, going right up onto your tiptoes, holding the stretch for 1 second.*

To continue
Repeat the exercise until you have done it 8 times.

1d

Exercise 2
Shoot the Eagle by
Drawing the Bow to
Each Side

2a *From the Starting position
(p.26), bend your knees a little
and raise your hands to chest
height, palms facing inward.
Your arms form an ellipse,
fingers pointing toward each
other.*

2b *Lower the left elbow and
turn the left hand around,
fingers pointing upward, palm
facing outward. Turn your head
to the left.*

2c *Imagine you are holding a
bowstring. Pull on the string,
drawing your right elbow back,
keeping the arm at shoulder
height. At the same time, push
your left hand out, palm facing
forward. Hold this stretch for 1
second, then relax. (See also
photograph, facing page.)*

To continue
*Repeat 2a-c on the right side of
the body. Continue to the left
side and to the right again,
performing the exercise 4 times
on each side.*

Position c from Exercise 2, Shoot the Eagle by Drawing the Bow to Each Side.

Exercise 3
Regulate Spleen and
Stomach by Raising Each
Hand

3a *From the Starting position
(p.26), move into 2a (p.28),
with your arms in front of you,
fingers pointing toward each
other. Then turn your left arm
at the elbow, raising the hand,
palm upward, fingers pointing
to your back. Lower the right
hand from the elbow, turning
your right palm downward.*

3b *Push your left hand up and
your right hand down fully.
Hold this stretch for 1 second.
Then let both arms relax.*

3a

3b

To continue
*Repeat the exercise on the other
side of the body. Perform the
exercise 4 times on each side.*

4a

Exercise 4
Cow Looks at the Moon
Behind

4a *From the Starting position
(p.26), raise your arms to chest
height, forming a horizontal
circle in front of you, with the
palms of your hands facing
inward (your arms further
forward than in 2a, p.28).
Turn your body to the left.*

4b *Continue moving your upper body to the left as far as you can while you raise your hands to face height, turning the palms to face outward. Hold this leftward stretch for 1 second.*

To continue
Relax, return the arms to the front, and repeat the movement on the right side. Do the exercise 4 times on each side.

4b

Exercise 5
Cool Excess Heat by Lowering the Head and Swinging the Hips

5a *Begin in the Starting position, then circle your right arm outward and upward, ending with the hand palm downward, above your head.*

5b *Bend sideways to your left, with your right arm curving over your head, so that both hands point to the ground. Allow your right heel to lift. Hold this for 1 second, and relax.*

5a

5b

To continue
Return the way you came, and repeat on the other side. Do this 4 times on each side.

Exercise 6
Strengthen the Kidneys and
Loins by Bending Forward
and Touching your Toes

6a *Begin in the Starting
position. Then circle both your
arms out to the sides, to
shoulder height, until both the
palms of your hands are facing
upward and tilted slightly
toward the front.*

6a

6b *Continue moving both arms
upward then forward and over,
until they are straight out in
front of you, palms downward,
about shoulders' width apart.*

6b

6c *As the arms continue their
downward arc, squat down as
low as you can, until your hands
touch your toes. Hold for 1
second, then stand up again, and
relax.*

To continue
*Repeat the exercise until you
have done it 8 times.*

6c

Exercise 7
Increase the Chi by Punching

Fist style for Exercise 7, thumbs inside fingers

7a *From the Starting position, bend your knees slightly. Make your hands into fists (see Fist style, above centre) and bring them up to hip level, palms up.*

7a

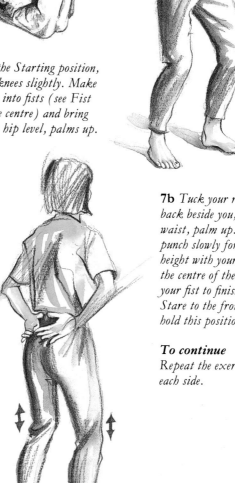

7b

7b *Tuck your right arm further back beside you, the fist by your waist, palm up. Meanwhile, punch slowly forward at chest height with your left fist, toward the centre of the body, turning your fist to finish palm down. Stare to the front of you, and hold this position for 1 second.*

To continue
Repeat the exercise 4 times on each side.

Exercise 8
Ward Off Illness by Shaking the Body

8 *From the Starting position, put your hands in the small of your back, palms outward. Lightly run the backs of your hands up and down your lower back, and shake your body up and down by flexing your knees. Continue this shaking while you inhale and exhale 8 times.*

8

Chi Kung

Once you have warmed up your body by practising Ba Duan Jin, you will be ready to start the more static Chi Kung exercises. These movements have been practised for thousands of years, evolving in response to triple needs: improved posture; better breathing; and greater concentration. At first sight they appear less vigorous than Ba Duan Jin, but this is deceptive. Though very easy to learn, they are in fact more demanding, and their effect on the performer can be profound. You should practise basic Chi Kung for about a year or so before attempting the Intermediate series (pp.37-41). Your breathing should remain completely natural during your practice session (p.25).

Basic Chi Kung
In the basic Chi Kung exercises you adopt a posture and hold it for several minutes, breathing naturally from the Tan Tien in the lower abdomen (p.24). You can perform the series either standing, as shown below, or sitting or lying down (p.36), whichever suits you best.

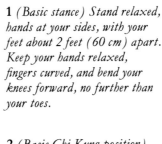

1 *(Basic stance) Stand relaxed, hands at your sides, with your feet about 2 feet (60 cm) apart. Keep your hands relaxed, fingers curved, and bend your knees forward, no further than your toes.*

2 *(Basic Chi Kung position) Raise your hands in front of you, with your fingers pointing to each other, about one hand's width apart. Try to feel light and buoyant, as if you were holding a balloon under each arm, or as if your arms were floating in water. At the same time, imagine that you are sitting on a balloon, and lightly gripping a balloon between your knees. Feel that your feet are sinking into the ground while your toes lightly grip the floor. And imagine that your hair is gently lifting your head, as if it were attached by string to the ceiling. Hold this position for about 5 minutes, keeping the floating and sinking sensations in your mind.*

1

2

3 *Move your arms downward and outward at both sides, so that your hands are at hip level, palms downward. Hold this position for about 2 minutes.*

3

4 *Steadily swing both arms upward in a complete circle, until your hands are in front of your face, palms facing outward and tilted upward, until you can see between your hands. Hold for about 2 minutes.*

4

5 *Circle both your arms outward and downward in an arc, until they are in front of the Tan Tien, the palms toward you. Hold this position for about 2 minutes.*

5

Sitting exercises

You can practise the basic exercises, 1-5, in a sitting position, if it suits you better. Choose a firm, straightbacked, armless chair rather than a soft-seated one. Keep your back upright but without tension, and place your feet flat on the floor, about shoulders' width apart. Sit upright. (The illustration on the left shows exercise 2, p.34, in the seated position.)

Lying-down exercises

Alternatively, practise exercises 1-5 while you are lying down. You should lie on the ground, or choose a firm surface, and put a thin pillow under your head and upper shoulders. Your toes should point upward. In position 3, just rest your hands palms up on the ground. In position 5 you can rest your hands on the Tan Tien rather than keep them above it. (The illustration on the right shows exercise 2 in the lying-down position.)

Intermediate Chi Kung

The following are more advanced exercises and should
only be practised after you have been performing the
basic exercises for a year or more. These movements
require a developed sense of balance, and a body that is
already flexible from practising the basic exercises, and
Ba Duan Jin. You should gradually increase the length
of time you hold the postures, from 1 up to 5 minutes.
As you become more familiar with the exercises, and as
your muscles strengthen and your limbs gain further
flexibility, you can start to try more advanced stretches,
such as those described in exercises 3 and 4.

Intermediate exercise 1

1a *Take up the Basic Chi Kung
position (p.34): your feet are a
little more than shoulders' width
apart, your knees bent forward
no further than your toes; your
hands are raised in front of you,
palms facing inward, fingers
pointing to each other. Transfer
your weight to your right foot
and turn a little to the left.
Point your left foot outward,
lifting the heel off the ground.*

1b *Open the fingers of both
hands, and point them slightly
downward and to your left.
Your legs should remain in the
same position. Hold this
position for at least 1 minute,
then return to the Basic Chi
Kung position.*

1a

1b

To continue
*Repeat 1a and 1b on the other
side of the body.*

2a

Intermediate exercise 2

2a *Repeat the movements of exercise 1 (p.37), moving to the left, but slide your left leg further outward (making about one-and-a-half times the space between your feet as in exercise 1). You should feel yourself to be well balanced, with more of your weight on your back foot. Check that your torso is upright. Place your hands about one-and-a-half times as far apart as in exercise 1.*

2b *Step back a little further with your right leg. Circle both your hands upward, then outward and down, turning the palms to face downward. Look down toward the ground. This posture is known as "Stopping the Balloon Flying".*

2b

To continue
Return to 2a and repeat exercise 2 on the other side of the body.

The advanced position, left leg forward, from Intermediate exercise 4.

Intermediate exercise 3
3a *From the Basic Chi Kung position (p.34), shift your weight onto your right leg and lift your left heel.*

3b *Imagining a string connecting your left hand with your left knee, raise your left hand in front of you and to the side, turning the palm outward. At the same time, raise your left knee up to waist level, keeping the sole of the foot parallel to the ground. As the left arm and leg rise, push your right hand down, palm down, fingers forward. Hold this posture for at least 1 minute. (See also photograph, p.22.)*

3a

To continue
Return to 3a and repeat the exercise on the other side.

3b

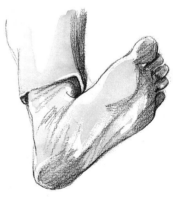

Advanced position 3b
When you are more experienced you can stretch the heel of the raised foot even more, pulling the toes up as far as possible.

4a

Intermediate exercise 4
4a *Starting from the basic Chi Kung position (p.34), but with your arms raised only as far as hip level, shift your weight onto your right leg, and raise your left heel.*

4b *Lift up your left foot and move it behind you and to the right so that it passes close behind the right calf.*

4b

4c *Put your left foot down on the ground behind you, with the toes pointing to your right heel. Then push your left hand forward, palm forward, in a parrying gesture, and push your right hand down, almost parallel to your left leg. Twist your body to the right and look at your left foot. In the more advanced version of 4c (see photograph, p.39) you place the back foot further behind and to the side, so there is a at least 3 feet (about a metre) between the heels, and the whole stance is substantially lower.*

4c

To continue
Return to 4a and repeat the exercise on the other side.

Chi Kung walk

After practising Chi Kung exercises your body may feel a little cool, stiff, or even a bit tired. To restore your circulation and relieve any aching in your limbs, you should complete your session with the Chi Kung walk.

Each of the soft arts has its own special walking system, designed to relax you and to help you perform that art in the best possible way. The more advanced forms of walking, those for Pa Kua (pp.67-71) and T'ai Chi Chuan (pp.88-9), also form the basic steps for their exercises. But the Chi Kung walk is the simplest of all.

Walking on ice in the dark

The walk should look and feel as if every step is momentous and slow – just like walking on thin ice, or like an astronaut's walk in space. Each step is in slow motion, and each movement is very carefully balanced. You should feel that you are almost lifting yourself off your feet, that you are as light as you can be, and that it is only your feet that can tell you if it is safe to go forward. It helps to hold your hands out to the sides, for finer balance. Before you start, gently shake your arms, letting them move loosely by your sides for a few minutes.

1a *Place your heels together, toes pointing outward, and put your arms in Chi Kung position 3 (p.35), out to the sides. Look straight ahead of you, and imagine that you are looking into the dark.*

1a

1b *Bend your knees slightly, then slowly shift your weight to your left leg, and lift your right foot up, just clear of the ground and parallel to it. Keep looking forward.*

1b

1c *Gently push your right leg forward and out to the side at about 30 or 45 degrees from centre. Try to feel as if you are rolling a pencil under your foot, but don't touch the ground.*

1d *Roll the imaginary pencil back to beside your left foot, without letting your right foot touch the ground.*

1c

1e *Curve your right foot behind you and outward, still rolling the pencil.*

1d

1e

1f *When your right leg tires, place it gently on the ground.*

To continue
Slowly transfer your weight to the right leg, and begin to explore space with the left foot in exactly the same way. Continue until it too gets tired.

1f

形意拳

2: Hsing I
Ways to harmony

At first glance, Hsing I looks like an external art; the movements are performed in a straight line, forward and back, with a variety of punches and kicks. But a closer look reveals that all its movements are rounded, and flowing is emphasized in their performance. In a way, the "hard" appearance of Hsing I is a camouflage which disguises its true depths, and even its name contains opposite meanings – "Hsing" means form, manifestation or outward appearance, while "I" means will, intention, or internal aim. So this art is concerned with controlling the body with the mind.

The practice of Hsing I is divided into two areas. First, some of the basic techniques which Hsing I uses are related to the Five Elements (p.46 and pp.150-1) – fundamental concepts that are translated here into human movements. Second, the more advanced forms of Hsing I are derived from the movements of twelve animals.

In China it is common for Hsing I and Pa Kua (Chapter 3, pp.64-81), to be taught together, but some masters hold that Hsing I is the first in a sequence that reflects the increasing complexity of the arts: Pa Kua is more complex than Hsing I; and T'ai Chi Chuan is the most advanced art of all.

Hsing I is deeply influenced by the philosophy of Taoism (p.12), which lies at the roots of all the soft arts, and over the centuries its philosophy has trans-formed them from their mechanistic fighting origins into profound forms of movement. At the heart of Taoism there is a profound reverence for nature in all its aspects, and this reverence is the cornerstone of the art. Although technically they are very advanced, the animal forms (p.60) best exemplify this aspect. Taoists believe that the key to understanding all things lies in the study of nature. By watching with minute care and attention the ways of the animals and plants, the earth and the heavens, you begin to understand them, and to see your own place in the order of things.

So it is through observing and imitating the external form of an animal – its "Hsing" – that understanding is born – you begin to understand its will or intention, the "I". Perhaps the first discovery of the new student is that it is the will or "I" that motivates you in the exercises. That is, the mind controls the body, and we must want to do something before we can do it. So if you are able to penetrate the "I" of yourself or of any other being in the universe, you have taken the first step toward a deeper understanding.

Hsing I is both a rigorous physical discipline and a profound form of moving meditation. It is this spiritual depth as much as its physical differences that distinguishes the soft arts from their cruder "hard" cousins like Kung Fu or Karate.

The Five Elements

The ancient Taoist founders of Hsing I observed with great care the movements of twelve animals, seeking the "I", the will or intention, in each one. They then converted their findings into human performance, the animal forms to which all Hsing I students aspire, shown in the final part of this chapter (pp.60-3). The aim is not to copy the animal's movements, however. The art requires that you imitate the "I" within the animal, and find the "I" within yourself. Learning Hsing I may thus become a process of internal revelation.

To help us reach this understanding, the creators of the art also invented a series of simpler exercises which contain the basic leg, arm, and body movements. The Five Element exercises (pp.48-59) include first a Commencing Form, and then turning and finishing steps which are also used in the animal forms. But these simpler exercises also have their deeper aspects, as each of them relates to one of the fundamental components of the universe. The Five Elements are Fire, Earth, Metal, Water, and Wood. In classical Chinese thought these elements are arranged in a clockwise cycle, as shown below. The Hsing I exercises, however, are not practised in exactly the same order. Instead, you start with Metal, and proceed to Wood, then Water, Fire, and Earth.

The elements in Hsing I
In Hsing I each element is assigned a specific function and a series of movements. Each one is associated with a specific organ in the body, and if you have a problem related to one of these organs you can improve your health by practising the relevant element exercise. Thus, for example, Metal is associated with the action of Splitting (like an axe), and is related to the lungs. The elements are arranged hierarchically, as shown in the diagram below, so that some overcome others.

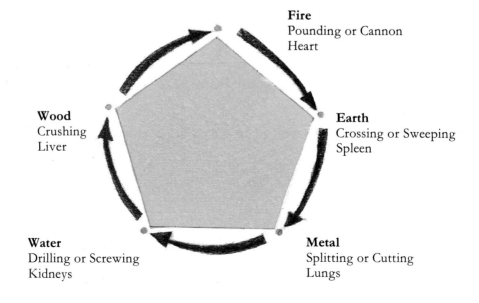

Fire
Pounding or Cannon
Heart

Wood
Crushing
Liver

Earth
Crossing or Sweeping
Spleen

Water
Drilling or Screwing
Kidneys

Metal
Splitting or Cutting
Lungs

The Commencing Form

The Commencing Form which opens all the exercises of the Five Elements is also known as San Ti or the Three Essentials. These are a sort of "body alphabet" designed to help the performer maintain the correct posture and alignment of limbs and torso throughout his or her practice. The Three Essentials are Heaven, or the Head; Earth, or the Hands; and Man, the feet. These three are divided into a further three parts: the Head controls the head, back, and waist; the Hands control the hands, elbows, and shoulders; the Feet control the feet, knees, and thighs. These relationships will help to guide you in the correct co-ordinated posture and movement of Hsing I. Position F in the Commencing Form (p.49) clearly demonstrates the correlation of limbs and torso moving within an exercise.

Heaven – Head — head
back
waist

Earth – Hands — hands
elbows
shoulders

Man – Feet — feet
knees
thighs

Standing posture
This posture is often taught as an initiating exercise in Hsing I. Apart from strengthening your arms and legs, it instils a feeling for correct alignment. Stand with your legs together (knees closed), and heels together, toes a little apart. Keep your knees slightly bent so that they align with your toes. Raise your arms as if you were about to embrace someone, but keep the hands at chest height, palms down, elbows slightly bent. Make your hands into "Tiger's mouths", separating your thumbs from your fingers. Beginners should hold this pose for no more than 2 minutes, gradually extending the time – some students hold the pose for up to half an hour. All the time, breathe naturally through your nose from the Tan Tien (p.24), and keep your tongue touching the roof of your mouth. This applies throughout the Hsing I exercises.

The Commencing Form
This sequence is the opening movement for all the Five Element exercises, but it can also be practised as an exercise in its own right. The form is usually performed quite vigorously and quickly, but take your time when you are learning. You should try to keep your movements relaxed, and breathe naturally through your nose and from the Tan Tien. Later you may acquire more speed – an expert will be able to do all the exercises in only 2 or 3 minutes. If you are using them remedially, perform them slowly and gently.

A

B

A *Start in the Standing posture (p.47), but with your toes further apart; your left foot should point straight forward, and your right foot outward at about 45 degrees from centre. Now turn your body slightly to the right and circle your arms upward and outward to both sides. Keep the arms bent at the elbows and your hands with thumbs separated from the fingers. This is known as the "Tiger's mouth" position. As your hands approach face height, fingers pointing up, turn the palms to face downward.*

B *Push your hands downward, so that the palms of the hands are horizontal, at the level of the Tan Tien. Bend your knees so that they are no further forward than your toes.*

C *Keeping your knees bent, make a fist with your right hand and start to bring it up toward chest height, turning it until the palm faces upward. Keep the fist loose, not clenched. (The fists in Hsing I are always soft, until the moment they strike.) Your left hand remains at the Tan Tien.*

C

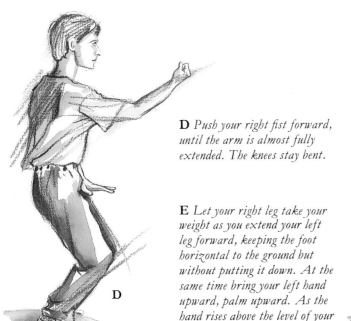

D *Push your right fist forward, until the arm is almost fully extended. The knees stay bent.*

E *Let your right leg take your weight as you extend your left leg forward, keeping the foot horizontal to the ground but without putting it down. At the same time bring your left hand upward, palm upward. As the hand rises above the level of your right elbow, turn the palm over.*

F *Slide your left hand over the top of your right forearm, until the arm is almost fully extended, palm forward. Drop your right hand, palm down, to the Tan Tien. Then put your left foot down on the ground. The standard pace in Hsing I measures about 3 feet (90 cm) from the heel of the back foot to the toes of the front foot (see also photograph, p.53).*

To *continue*

To practise the form as an individual exercise, repeat A-F on the other side of the body. Keep repeating the sequence on the left and then the right, moving straight ahead until you reach the limits of your space. Then turn, using the steps on page 51. (This can be done for a few minutes or an hour or so.) Otherwise, proceed from position F to the next element.

Splitting (Metal)

The arm movements here imitate the rising and falling action of an axe chopping. Your Chi (p.24 and p.150), or vital energy, rises and falls with your hands. According to the Chinese theory of the Five Elements (see also pp.151-3), Metal benefits the Lungs.

1a *From the end of the Commencing Form, position F, bring your left hand down, forming a fist at the level of the Tan Tien, the palm upward. Your right hand remains at the same level, palm down. Your left leg stays forward, with your weight resting on the right leg.*

1b *Shift forward onto your left leg. Push your left fist forward and up at shoulder height. As you move forward into 1c, make a brief, gentle stamping movement with your left foot, lifting it just off the ground and turning it outward. (This is characteristic of Hsing I).*

1c *Move further forward onto your left leg, and bring your right foot up beside it, keeping it about an inch (2 cm) above the ground. Meanwhile, raise your right hand and bring it to beside your left elbow. Open your left hand, palm upward.*

1d *Step forward onto your right leg, using the standard Hsing I pace (about 3ft or 90 cm from left heel to right toe). Your right foot points forward, your left swivels outward. Your right hand moves forward, while your left hand sinks down.*

1d

To continue
Repeat this sequence of steps, 1a-d, but lead with the other leg and arm. Continue in a straight line. To turn, use the steps described below. To end, use the steps on pp.57-8.

Turning steps
Use the leading foot – the one that was forward in your last step – to swivel the body around. If you led with your right foot, simply reverse the directions here.

1 *Turn your left foot inward as far as you can, pivoting it on the heel. Transfer your weight to the right leg, and swivel the right foot outward. At the same time bring both hands down to the Tan Tien.*

2 *Shift your weight to the left leg, and lift up your right foot, toes pointing up and outward. (This move is also shown on p.59.) To continue Splitting, make a fist with your right hand and raise it.*

1

2

Crushing (Wood)

To practise Crushing, start with the Commencing Form (pp.48-9), moving from F to 2a below. Wood is said to be able to expand and contract simultaneously – like the fist here, which is soft, then hard, then soft again. The crushing exercise is good for the Liver.

2a

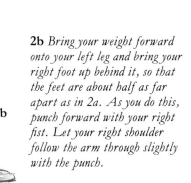

2b

2a *From the Commencing Form, lower your left hand, and make a fist with it. At the same time make a fist with your right hand, so that both hands are at the Tan Tien. Your legs remain in the same position, with the left leg forward, about 3 feet (90 cm) from the back heel to the front toe.*

2b *Bring your weight forward onto your left leg and bring your right foot up behind it, so that the feet are about half as far apart as in 2a. As you do this, punch forward with your right fist. Let your right shoulder follow the arm through slightly with the punch.*

To continue

Continue leading with the left foot, but alternate the punches with the right and left arms. Proceed in a straight line, using the Turning steps (p.51), when necessary, and close with the Finishing steps (pp.57-8).

Position F from the Commencing Form.

Drilling (Water)

The Drilling (or Screwing) title refers to the forward punch. This fast, forward movement is said to make the Chi "shoot like a geyser" or "streak like lightning". The water exercise is associated with the Kidneys.

3a *Start with the Commencing Form, A-F. Move to 2a (p.52). Then push your left fist forward, up and toward the centre of the body. This is the "Drilling" punch. Lift your left foot up briefly, turn it slightly outward and put it down again. Your right fist stays low.*

3a

3b *Open out both hands, left palm toward your face, right palm downward. Briefly raise your left foot, turning it outward as you move into 3c.*

3c *Step forward with your right leg. Raise the right arm, and form a fist, palm up. Lower the left hand, letting it slide down the underside of the right forearm, ending palm down.*

To continue
Alternate left and right. Use the Turning steps (p.51) and close with the Finishing steps (pp.57-8).

3b

3c

Pounding (Fire)

Pounding, also known as Cannon, symbolizes the explosive quality of Fire, as opposed to its heating or melting properties. The fists explode outward, one after the other, with a strong circular action. Like Fire, Pounding relates to the Heart – in China the exercise is commonly used by people with heart problems for its therapeutic benefits.

4a *Begin with the Commencing Form (pp.48-9). From position F, bring your right leg up beside your left leg. Your knees should be in line with your toes. Lower your left hand, palm down, beside your right. At the same time, turn your torso 45 degrees to the right.*

4a

4b *Step forward with your right leg, so that the shin is vertical and the thigh sloping. Bring your left leg closer to your right, to about half the standard pace, pointing the foot outward. At the same time, make your right hand into a fist, and bring it upward to just above your head, turning it outward so that the knuckles face backward. As you do this your left hand also makes a fist and punches forward at chest height.*

To continue

Alternate left and right. Use the Turning steps (p.51) and close with the Finishing steps (pp.57-8).

4b

Crossing (Earth)

Crossing or Sweeping applies to the arms – each fist in turn sweeps forward, crossing the other arm. The arms in 5a are both parrying and striking. The Chi is said to "strike forward with rounded energy". The fifth element, Earth, is related to the Spleen.

5a *As usual, start with the Commencing Form (pp.48-9). From F, move your left leg further forward to the left. Your toes should point slightly inward. Bring your right foot up to the left, but keep it hovering, with the sole parallel to the ground. Circle your right arm across your body, bringing it in toward the centre and upward, under your left arm. Make a fist and continue to raise it to chin level, palm up. As you do this, lower your left hand, forming a fist at the Tan Tien, palm down.*

5b *Step forward and to the right with your right foot. Bring your left foot up behind the right, as in 4b (p.55). As you do this, circle your left arm across your body, and under the right arm, making a fist which ends up at chin height, with the palm facing upward. At the same time, lower your right hand to the Tan Tien, and make a fist, palm down.*

To continue

Repeat 5a and 5b, alternating left and right. Use the Turning steps (p.51) when necessary, and close with the following Finishing steps.

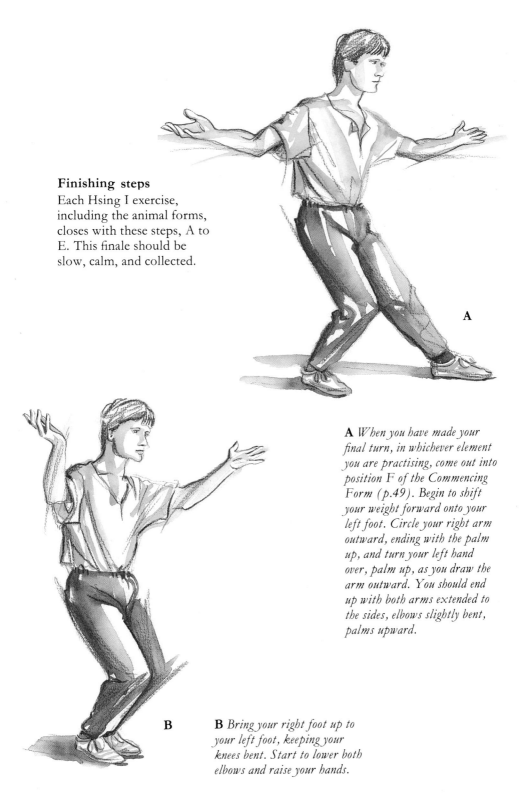

Finishing steps
Each Hsing I exercise, including the animal forms, closes with these steps, A to E. This finale should be slow, calm, and collected.

A

A *When you have made your final turn, in whichever element you are practising, come out into position F of the Commencing Form (p.49). Begin to shift your weight forward onto your left foot. Circle your right arm outward, ending with the palm up, and turn your left hand over, palm up, as you draw the arm outward. You should end up with both arms extended to the sides, elbows slightly bent, palms upward.*

B

B *Bring your right foot up to your left foot, keeping your knees bent. Start to lower both elbows and raise your hands.*

C *Circle both your arms over and in toward the centre line of your body and down, lowering your posture a little more. This gathers the Chi and brings it down. Take both hands down to the Tan Tien, palms facing downward. At the lowest point, twist your torso slightly to the left — in action this becomes a slight wriggle which helps to settle the Chi.*

C

D

D *Now raise yourself upward, straightening your legs, twisting the torso slightly to the right so that you are standing straight again. At the same time let your arms come back to your sides, unbending the elbows.*

E

E *Slowly go up onto your tiptoes, then back down. Finally, stand still for a few moments, breathing deeply and evenly from the Tan Tien.*

Step 2 from the Turning steps.

The Twelve Animals

In Hsing I, each animal inspires a movement that imitates its outer form and embodies its spirit and perceived intention. The exercises – Dragon, Tiger, Monkey, Horse, Crocodile (or Turtle), Cock (or Chicken), Sparrowhawk (or Falcon), Swallow, Snake, Crane (Dove), Eagle, and Bear – appear almost balletic, but in fact they are intended to add variety of technique in the fighting discipline. They are much more advanced and complicated than the Five Element forms. Only the Tiger is taught here in step-by-step detail, since it is one of the more straightforward forms. Most of the other forms are very advanced – Hsing I masters generally teach only one or two. The Eagle, Dragon, and Swallow are shown on page 62; the Horse and Monkey appear on pages 44 and 63.

Each animal form is preceded by the Commencing Form (pp.48-9) and the action repeated again and again, the performer moving in straight lines, as usual in Hsing I.

Tiger
The tiger is the most powerful and aggressive animal in China. This form feels more tigerish than it looks – its "I" is more important than its "Hsing". The tiger's strike is expressed in the pouncing movements of the hands. In a variant interpretation the hands and forearms imitate the opening and closing of the tiger's jaws.

1a *From position* F *in the Commencing Form (p.49) – left leg forward, left arm raised with the hand in a fist palm upward, right arm down at the Tan Tien – step forward and to the left onto the left foot. Bring your right arm up parallel to your left arm, with your hands open and stretching forward.*

1b *Bring your right leg up to beside your left, and push both hands down to the Tan Tien.*

1c *Make both hands into fists, palms down, gathering the Chi to take it up, and then turn them over so the palms face inward, pulling your elbows back slightly.*

1c

1d *Step forward and slightly to the right with your right leg, but without putting your foot down. Bring both your fists up and cross them in front of you at shoulder level, palms inward, the left inside the right.*

1d

1e *Now step onto the right foot and bring your left foot closer to it. Open both hands, palms to the front, and push them forward, with your fingers flexed. Let your wrists rub together and then separate again. The action of the hands is said to be "ripping".*

1e

To continue
Repeat the action of 1a-e, but on the other side of the body, and continue alternating left and right, proceeding in a straight line. Use the Turning steps (p.51) when you reach the end of your individual space, and close with the Finishing steps (pp.57-8).

Eagle

The eagle's movement is a straightforward plunging and grasping assault on its prey. Expert performers practise the Eagle form by lifting huge stone jars from their uppermost rims. Another Hsing I animal, the Falcon, or Sparrowhawk, displays a similar swooping predatory movement.

Dragon

The Dragon is known for its vigour and its alarming leaping and bouncing movements. The Hsing I form has the beast crouching and creeping, then jumping vertically, with great alacrity and strength.

Swallow

The arms mimic the bird's graceful wing span and swooping flight. The form is fast and full of surprise. The performer swoops down – and, in combat, up-ends the opponent by grabbing his or her ankle and pulling it forward.

The Monkey form, one of the Twelve Animals.

八卦掌

3: Pa Kua

Eternal change

To look at, Pa Kua is perhaps the strangest of all the martial arts, soft or hard, internal or external. The performer moves at high speed, whirling around in circles, suddenly changing direction, swooping up and down, changing again and so on. At first this rapid circling looks totally unrelated to Hsing I or T'ai Chi Chuan. Yet it shares with them common roots, both in its outer form, its philosophical roots, and its inner meaning (see Origins and philosophies of the arts, pp.12-14).

Pa Kua literally means eight diagrams and refers to the eight simple patterns of parallel lines used in the classic Chinese text the *I Ching*, or the Book of Changes – an ancient compendium from various sources, some dating as far back as 800 BC (see also p.13, and p.66). As with T'ai Chi Chuan, the historical records of the performance of Pa Kua only go back about 300 years, but the philosophy behind it is nearly 3,000 years old. It is most likely that Pa Kua was passed down secretly from master to student for generations before it was first recorded (p.16), as is the case with the other soft martial arts.

The central essence of this art is change – and performing it is known as "doing the changes". Among the most important ideas in the philosophy of Taoism, on which Pa Kua is based, is the belief that all things in nature are in a state of constant and eternal change. And it is only by accepting this state of permanent flux that we can understand the reality of the world. This belief carries with it the idea that any attempt to impose a fixed form or structure, or an immutable shape, is ultimately false – an illusion born of the inability to come to terms with the transient nature of the Universe, and of human life itself.

While at first Pa Kua may seem rather obscure, it is not just a set of movements based on esoteric ideas. In fact, it is also highly effective in practice. And although it is true that when you learn Pa Kua you must initially take its form and structure into your movements, the main aim – which Pa Kua shares with all other soft arts – is the ultimate loss of form. The Pa Kua forms tend to be hard to learn precisely because they try to be as unpredictable as possible. The performer uses the knowledge that anyone who relies upon preformed ways of moving will be vulnerable to an opponent who knows these forms, for every movement will be predictable. The Pa Kua master reacts to events as they unfold and constantly changes form, thus baffling the opponent. And as his or her command of the art develops, he or she begins to lose form altogether, and thus becomes both utterly unpredictable, and closer to the natural self. In this way, Pa Kua endows the master with the ability to change and react instinctively and naturally in response to the other changes that affect us as we move through life.

The eight diagrams

The term Pa Kua actually means eight diagrams, or trigrams, and refers to the eight different designs of parallel lines used in the ancient *I Ching*, or Book of Changes – a classic text which is concerned with divining the future through games of chance (see also p.13). It is said that people used the diagrams to interpret the patterns formed when they threw dried yarrow stalks to the ground. Over the centuries the Book of Changes grew and developed into a rich storehouse of traditional Chinese knowledge and wisdom, not only of oracles and magic but of the roots of Chinese culture itself. And gradually the importance of the diagrams developed too. They emerged as symbols not of static concepts but of changing transitional states.

In the soft arts the diagrams are imagined in a circle laid out on the ground, which the performer follows during practice. Changes take place on each of the eight faces. There is a sense in which Pa Kua is an enactment of the constant drama of change that is the driving force of nature itself throughout the cosmos.

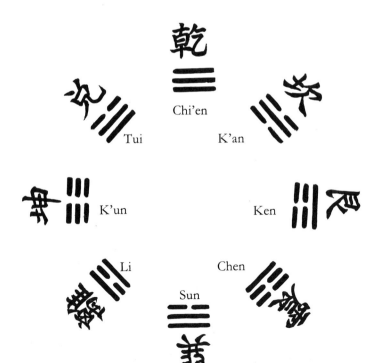

The eight trigrams
Each trigram has a title indicating its tendency in movement. In clockwise sequence from the top, Chi'en is Creative, K'an is Abysmal, Ken is Keeping Still, Chen is Arousing, Sun is Gentle, Li is Clinging, K'un is receptive, and Tui is Joyous.

Pa Kua walking

There are no special warming-up exercises for Pa Kua, as in Hsing I, but most students practise the walk before going on to the more complex forms. The walk shown below is the basis for all the following exercises. It strengthens the legs and promotes flexibility in the ankles – particularly important in the context of the rapid circling and changing movements you learn later on. It also helps to give you a feel for correct posture – in particular the foot hovering parallel to the ground.

Pa Kua walking
Start slowly and gradually increase speed, breathing naturally from the Tan Tien (p.24). Glide swiftly and smoothly in a straight line.

1a *Stand upright, with your feet together and arms by your sides. Look straight ahead.*

1b *Move your right leg forward, placing the foot flat on the ground, bending your left knee a little. Shift your weight onto your right leg.*

1c *Lift your left foot a bare inch (2 cm) off the ground, keeping the sole parallel to the ground.*

1d *Bring your left foot smoothly past your right foot, and move it forward, placing it flat on the ground.*

To continue
Shift your weight forward and continue, using the walking turn (p.68) when necessary.

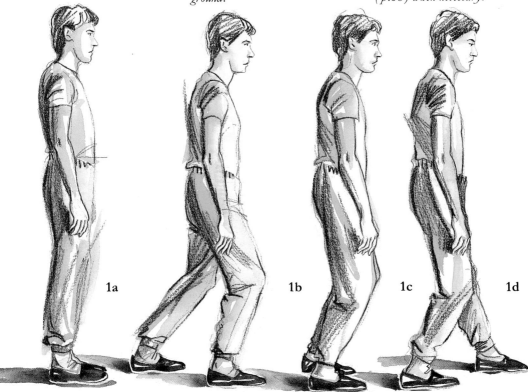

1a   1b   1c   1d

Pa Kua walking turn
Once you have reached the limits of your practice area walking in a straight line, you will need to take two turning steps. The steps below lead with the right foot – if you were leading with the left foot, simply reverse the directions.

2 *Bring your right foot off the ground, barely an inch (2 cm), and place it in front of the left, and at right angles to it, toes inward. Your knees should stay slightly bent in the knock-kneed stance that is typical of Pa Kua. This move is known as "stepping inward".*

3 *Shift your weight onto the right leg, then lift your left foot just off the ground and turn it right around to the left through 180 degrees.*

To continue
Shift your weight onto your left leg, swivelling your right foot until it is parallel to your left. You are now ready to continue Pa Kua walking.

1 *Starting the turn with your right leg forward, shift your weight back onto your left leg.*

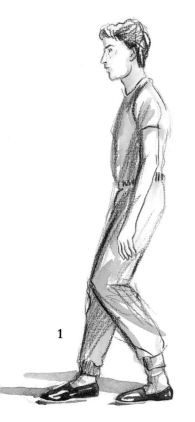

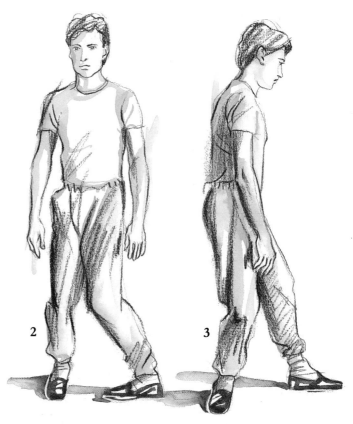

1

2

3

Position 1 from the Eight Fixed Postures.

Walking in a circle

You begin to enact the wisdom of the I Ching, the Book of Changes, when you start to walk the circle. The first steps are preparatory, and the actual circle starts at 2d. You can walk in a clockwise or counterclockwise direction. The size of your circle will depend on the available space, but on average the beginner takes about 8 steps. From 2d onward, you can adopt any one of the arm positions shown on pp.72-4 (the position shown below is the first of the eight). In martial application the circling allows you to surprise and evade your opponent.

2a *Stand relaxed, with your feet shoulders' width apart and your arms at your sides.*

2a

2b

2b *Circle your arms upward and outward, at the same time turning your body slightly to the right. Look ahead of you and to the right.*

2c *Circle your arms downward, with your hands in front of you, palms down, and fingers pointing toward each other (this is the first of the fixed arm positions, p.72). Now you are ready to start the circle.*

2c

2d *For the clockwise circle, turn your body slightly to the left as you shift your weight to your right leg, and put your left leg forward, with your foot just off the ground. Keep your arms in the same position.*

2d

2e

2e *Put your left foot down, turning the toes slightly inward, and shift your weight forward.*

2f *Lift your right foot, bringing it close by your left leg, keeping it parallel to the ground.*

2f

To continue
Proceed in a circle, using the same steps as in the straight line walk (p.67), but always turning the toes of the outside foot (the left if you are circling clockwise as above) inward.

The Eight Fixed Postures

These eight arm positions, performed while you are walking in a circle (pp.70-1), are important for your health, since each one moves the Chi or vital energy in a different direction, affecting different organs and meridians (p.152). You can do all of them in sequence or choose just one for your practice session. Try to concentrate on your arms as you move, encouraging the Chi to move freely, while at the same time training your mind and toning up your muscles. It helps if you focus your mind on the positions of your arms, and keep an awareness of the position's title, imagining yourself in the action it suggests. You can maintain each posture for anything from a few minutes to an hour or more, circling in a clockwise or counterclockwise direction.

The Eight Fixed Postures
The arm positions shown here apply to the clockwise circle. If you are circling in the opposite direction, you should reverse the arm positions, reading left for right and vice versa.

1 Press Down
Push your hands out in front of you, palms downward, fingers pointing toward each other. Imagine that you are holding a beach ball just under the surface of the sea, at around hip height, and pushing it down. The energy is said to be pushing down and forward (See also photograph, p.69.)

2 Embrace
Raise your arms in front of you, the right hand a little above the left – as if you were holding something very precious and, at the same time, pushing the world away from you.

1

2

3 Push Forward
Bring both arms up in front of you in a broken circle, then turn your hands around so that the palms face forward. Imagine that you are pushing something heavy away from you. Here the energy moves directly forward.

4 Hold Up the Heavens
Lift both arms out to the sides with your hands at head height, palms upward. You are exerting force outward and upward – your energy is said to expand outward.

5 Lion Plays Ball
Lift your left arm high over your head and curve the hand over toward the right. Extend your right hand to the side at about shoulder height, with the palm facing upward – as if you were tossing a ball from one hand to the other.

6 Push to the Front and Back
Curve your right hand in front of you at about shoulder height, twisting the palm to face forward. Put your left arm behind you with the hand at about waist height, and twist it so that palm faces outward. In this position, your energy is said to expand forward and backward, and upward and downward at the same time.

6

7 Join Heaven and Earth
Raise your right arm, with your fingers pointing straight to the sky. Bring your left hand down and across your body, fingers pointing to the ground. Your arms are forming a circuit between Heaven and Earth.

7

8 Dragon Turns its Waist
Move both arms to the right, with the right hand at about head height, the palm facing right, and the left hand beneath the right elbow, palm facing right. As you are walking, your hands are pushing into the centre of the clockwise circle. (See also photograph, p.64.)

8

Lion Plays Ball, position 5 from the Eight Fixed Postures.

Palm Changes

The Single and Double Palm Changes are usually performed when you want to change direction in either the straight line or the circular walk (p.67 and pp.70-1), and they are used between different arm postures. The movements shown here contain both the defensive and offensive techniques of Pa Kua – you learn how to execute the "kill" – as swiftly and efficiently as possible. Within the changes, the techniques for hitting, for dislocating limbs, for throttling and so forth are all disguised. There are many variations to both the single and double changes, but the two versions taught here contain the essential moves.

The Single Palm Change shown below and on page 78 involves a strike to the upper chest, followed by a strike to the head – an attack that brings your body around in a half circle. The Double Palm Change (pp.80-1) involves the techniques of the single change and a further series of blows – at the same time turning your body through 360 degrees.

3a

Single Palm Change

3a(4a) *Start with your arms in the Press Down position of the Eight Fixed Postures (p.72). As you walk forward onto your right foot – in the straight line or the circular walk – curve your right arm inward and upward to face height, and bring your left hand up toward your right elbow, palm up. Turn your head toward the right.*

3b(4b) *Turn your whole body to the right and turn your hands outward to the right. Keep your left hand below your right elbow.*

3b

3c(4c) *Bring your left foot up beside your right foot, turning the heel outward so it is at right angles to the right foot. Rotate your body to the right with this movement.*

3c

3d(4d) *Now lift your right foot just off the ground, and turn the toes through 90 degrees to the right. Turn your right hand down, as if to parry a blow, with the palm forward.*

3d

3e(4e) *Step forward and to the right with your right foot shifting your weight forward slightly. Push your right hand further forward.*

3f(4f) *Step forward with the left foot and turn the toes in toward the right foot, at right angles to it. Bring your left hand right across your body, palm upward, then draw both arms close in to your body, turning your right hand so that the palm faces upward.*

3e

3f

3g *Turn your body back to the left, taking your left arm out to the side, and turning the hand so that the palm faces outward. At the same time, bring your right hand across the body until it is almost under your left elbow, turning it so that the palm faces outward. As you finish this arm movement, shift your weight backward onto your right foot and turn your left foot through 90 degrees to the left. The arm position is the same as fixed posture 8. (See also photograph, p.64.)*

3g

To continue
Return to the circular or straight line walk, continuing with the same arm position or changing to the next one.

Position 4i from the Double Palm Change.

Double Palm Change

The double change contains the first six steps of the single change. The closing movements below take you through a further 180 degrees, completing a full turn.

4g *Perform 4a-f (pp.76-8), the single change. Then, from position 4f, with your left arm under your right arm, and your toes toward each other, transfer your weight onto your left foot and spin around to the left, bringing your right foot up to your left foot. Push your left arm straight up, palm to the right, and your right arm down and across your body.*

4g

4h *Turn to the right and lift the right heel a little. At the same time, bring both arms together, crossing them at the wrist, left over right.*

4h

4i *Take a wide step to the right, lowering your stance, and separate your arms, pushing them out to the sides, palms downward.*

4i

4j *Now bring your left leg up to your right, placing your left foot, toes inward, at right angles to your right foot. Bring both arms close to your body, the left arm under your right arm, hands palms upward.*

4k *Swivel your left foot outward turning your body to the left. Push both your arms to the left, the left hand extended, palm facing forward, the right across your lower body. The arm position is the same as fixed posture 8.*

4j

To continue
Move your arms into your chosen fixed posture and continue your circular or straight line walking.

4k

太極拳

4: T'ai Chi Chuan
The art of awareness

To those experienced in the soft arts, T'ai Chi Chuan is the ultimate art. In fact, "T'ai" means ultimate or supreme, while "Chi" (which in this context has a different tone to the word for energy) means "polarity", as in the extremes of North and South. In T'ai Chi Chuan, this polarity refers to the extremes of Yin and Yang, light and shade. "Chuan" literally means the fist, but is conventionally translated as boxing or "the fist way". T'ai Chi Chuan is thus Supreme Pole Boxing. As the sublime achievement in the soft martial arts, this is a subtle, sophisticated, and effective system of self defence, though its practice takes you beyond the martial aspects of the art.

Deriving from the oldest Taoist principles, T'ai Chi Chuan has a relatively brief recorded history (p.17). The movements it contains can all be found in the ancient texts of Chi Kung and other early forms of Chinese exercise, but the earliest existing records of independent practice come from about 200 years ago.

In China, and increasingly throughout the rest of the world, T'ai Chi Chuan is recognized for its great powers in instilling and maintaining good health and fitness in people of all ages. Regular practice prevents the onset of illness, and can prove effective in the treatment of common ailments and debilitating conditions. As all T'ai Chi exercise is practised slowly, no oxygen debt builds up during practice – so this art is suitable for many people who suffer chronic illnesses, such as high blood pressure. The Chinese authorities recently carried out fitness tests on a group of regular practitioners of the Short Form, comparing their health and fitness with that of a similar group of non-practitioners. They found that the T'ai Chi students had more efficient circulatory and respiratory systems and metabolisms. Other clinical tests have shown that T'ai Chi can also be very beneficial for people suffering from insomnia, anxiety, or debilitating psychological states. One simple but profound reason for this is that to do the Short Form you have to concentrate continuously for the time it takes to perform it. The concentration required does wonders in calming the mind. And practising T'ai Chi induces a deep sense of calm and well-being.

Finally, sustained practice of T'ai Chi is in itself a form of spiritual training. Perhaps more than any other soft art, the forms of T'ai Chi are like moving meditation. They require complete concentration, and they help to instil this in the student; they require an absolutely empty mind, devoid of feelings or intention, and they give that to the student too. And over time they instil a rhythm and a sense of detachment, which once found is never lost and always valued. T'ai Chi Chuan repays all the efforts you put into it, with interest.

Governing principles

T'ai Chi Chuan brings together and re-evaluates many of
the principles that it shares with Chi Kung, Hsing I, and
Pa Kua. Among the most important of these is the idea
of harmonizing opposites, or bringing together and
controlling opposing forces. The term T'ai Chi refers to
the opposite poles of the Yin Yang symbol, and the
symbol (right) is perfectly balanced or harmonized. This
harmonizing of opposites is true too in the performance
of the art itself. The essence of T'ai Chi is that in softness
there is also firmness, in yielding there is strength. Some
of the titles used to describe the steps in the Short Form
express these opposites with poetic symbolism – for
example, Step 7 is sometimes known as Grasping the
Sparrow's Tail while Warding Off the Tiger.

The *Tao Te Ching*, written by the sage Lao Tzu over
2,000 years ago (see also p.13), contains the essential
philosophy:

*The weakest things in the world can overmatch the strongest
   things in the world.*
*Nothing in the world can be compared to water for its weak and
   yielding nature; yet in attacking the hard and strong nothing
   proves better than it. For there is no other alternative to it.*
*The weak can overcome the strong and the yielding can overcome
   the hard:*
This all the world knows but does not practise.

These words of Lao Tzu use the images of the Five
Elements (p.151) and of the meeting of opposites. They
give the essence of T'ai Chi in a few short, poetic
sentences.

The T'ai Chi symbol
The symbol which most
people in the West know as
the Yin Yang symbol is also
known as the T'ai Chi
symbol. The black area is
the Yang, the white area the
Yin. Each of the extremes,
or poles, contains the seeds
of its opposite – hence the
black dot in the white part
and the white dot in the
black part. The black area
embraces the white area,
and vice versa.

Yielding, rootedness, and expulsion
In practice, this means that T'ai Chi Chuan achieves its
efficiency as a self-defence system by combining
opposing tendencies. If a T'ai Chi adept is attacked, the
first action will be to yield before the attacker. In
yielding, the defender turns his or her own movements
into harmony with, rather than in opposition to, the
direction of the attacker's force. But this does not mean
that the defender is struck down or knocked out of the
way. On the contrary, T'ai Chi training instils agility,
balance, and control – the defender takes a rooted stance
that enables him or her to remain firm and in control,

and to use the force of the opponent's attack to unbalance and repel him or her.

Anyone making an attack is essentially performing an external act of aggression, a burst of forward-moving energy usually concentrated in one hand or foot. At the moment of release of energy the aggressor is therefore at least temporarily out of control. This is the point when the T'ai Chi adept reacts.

T'ai Chi Chuan teaches a number of ways to expel the energy of the aggressor, for instance, by pushing, locking or throwing, using pressure against the joints, or on sensitive points on the body. The aim is to achieve expulsion with minimal force – the Chinese say that the expert "wards off 1,000 lb with the force of 4 ounces". T'ai Chi also makes use of a variety of kicks, punches, and other blows, but most of them are designed to neutralize attack without inflicting serious injury. These techniques are built into the T'ai Chi Short Form, and some of them are demonstrated in the section toward the end of this chapter on Basic Powers and Pushing Hands.

Mastering the Chi

T'ai Chi Chuan is based on many principles and beliefs. Like the other soft arts it is deeply concerned with Chi (p.24), the vital energy that flows through the body, and it aims to bring balance to body, mind, and spirit – through specially devised movements, natural deep breathing, and a calm state of mind. The 24-step Short Form, which forms the greater part of this chapter, is a simplified version of T'ai Chi, but it will bring all of these benefits to those who perform it regularly. Many Chinese practise these exercises outside under the trees in the early morning, where the natural Chi is thought to be most potent, and readily absorbed by the performer. Some masters say that practising in the evening is particularly good for the brain. Whatever the circumstances, you should try to practise when you feel you will get the greatest benefit. If you can't practise outside on a regular basis you may be able to take advantage of a particularly sunny day, or a scenic spot with fresh, unpolluted air. In this way you will be taking good things into your body and your mind.

Warming up

Some people like to start a session of T'ai Chi with warming-up exercises. This is not essential – in theory you should be constantly ready to perform T'ai Chi in self defence. And since the Short Form, the most important exercise in this chapter, is itself a systematic programme for stretching the body, starting gently and steadily becoming more demanding, it can be performed safely with no prior preparation.

In practice though, many people prefer to start a martial arts' session with some gentle stretching exercises (hence the pairing of Ba Duan Jin and Chi Kung in Chapter 1), and T'ai Chi has its own set of warming-up movements. These are designed to loosen and tone all the major muscle groups used in T'ai Chi, and to massage the internal organs, as well as maintaining general health. Some of the exercises may also be used for specific therapeutic purposes.

1 With your feet together, bend your knees slightly, put your hands on your knees, and then slowly rotate them, 5 times to the left and 5 times to the right. This gently loosens all the tendons which meet at the knee, and can be helpful for sufferers of arthritis of the knee.

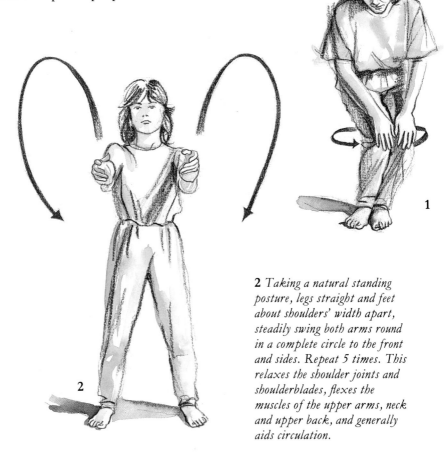

1

2

2 Taking a natural standing posture, legs straight and feet about shoulders' width apart, steadily swing both arms round in a complete circle to the front and sides. Repeat 5 times. This relaxes the shoulder joints and shoulderblades, flexes the muscles of the upper arms, neck and upper back, and generally aids circulation.

3

3 *First raise your hands to shoulder height, palms down. Then squat down as low as you can, holding your arms out in front of you as counterweights. Repeat 5 times. This works the muscles and joints of your hips, knees, and ankles, and tones the muscles of your lower back. Holding the arms horizontal also tones their muscles.*

4 *Standing as in exercise 2, with the backs of your hands on your hips, turn your body and head to the left, looking up. Return to the front and repeat to the right. Repeat 5 times. This rotates the spine and opens up the ribcage.*

4

5

5 *With your right hand, pick up your right leg, pulling the knee toward your chest, while the left hand pulls the right foot upward. Return your foot to the floor and repeat on the left side. Repeat 5 times on each side. This stretches a different set of leg tendons to exercise 1, and works the muscles of your upper and lower arms.*

T'ai Chi walking

This is the basic method for all the foot movements in T'ai Chi, and it is a good way for the beginner to get a feel for the right posture and rhythm of the movements that you adopt when you perform the Short Form on pages 91-139. You can practise T'ai Chi walking as a separate drill, moving rhythmically across your room or training area, continuing for as long as you like. This develops your sense of balance and gives a deep sense of rootedness and security. All moves should be slow and even, with no pauses between the steps. Once you have mastered this you will be in control of all the lower body movements of the Short Form. If your legs are stiff, try the warming-up exercises on pages 86-7. While you are practising the walk, keep your eyes looking forward and downward – not staring, but focused and aware. Your torso should stay upright, and your movements smooth, without any bobbing of the head and shoulders.

The take-up posture (left)
Start by standing with your heels together and your toes turned slightly outward. Breathe from the Tan Tien (p.24) in the lower abdomen. Your weight should be evenly distributed, and your feet should "feel" the ground. Breathing slowly and naturally, place your hands lightly on your hips, palms inward. Let your knees sink downward.

1a

T'ai Chi walking

1a *From the take-up posture, facing page, move your left leg forward and slightly outward, as if you were skating on ice, but in slow motion. Place your left heel on the ground, without shifting your balance, leaving your weight on the right leg. Your gaze remains straight ahead of you and downward.*

1b *Put your left foot down fully and transfer your weight onto the left leg, keeping the left knee slightly bent (the knee no further forward than the toes), while the right leg straightens.*

1c *Slowly begin to raise your right foot and bend the knee as you bring the right leg toward the left leg, keeping the heel up.*

1d *Continue moving of your right leg forward and slightly to the right, placing the right heel on the ground.*

To continue

Transfer your weight to your right leg, and bring your left foot, heel up, to beside your right foot. Repeat steps 1-4. Take care to check that you are moving at an even, smooth pace.

The walking turn

When you have gone as far as you can in one direction, begin to step forward but turn the leading foot inward at an angle of 45 degrees. Pivot it on the heel, leaving your weight on the back leg. Then transfer your weight onto your foot, at the same time twisting your hips to follow the leading foot. Swivel your back foot around, through 180 degrees, and turn your body further, so that you are facing the way you came, and you can continue your T'ai Chi walking.

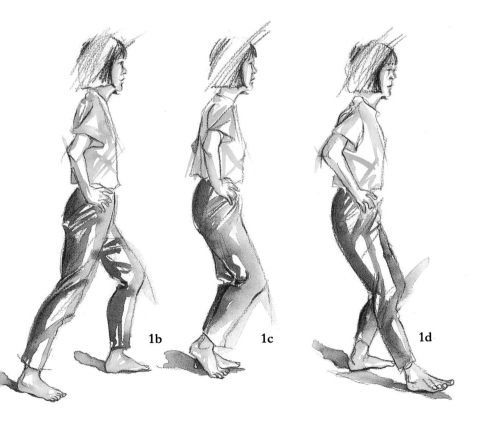

1b   1c   1d

The Short Form

This is the best known T'ai Chi exercise, a continual flow of movements that is divided into 24 steps for teaching purposes. Derived from the longer forms of T'ai Chi, it takes only 5 minutes or so to perform. Although each of the 24 steps is named, when practised by a master there is no pause, no change in pace, no beginning or end of the step. Instead there is a continual steady movement from one step to the next, from the beginning to the very end. The official Chinese instruction manual gives a perfect description of this seamless movement:

"While making a stride, it is as quietly as a cat walks, and while putting forth strength the exertion is so mild that it looks like reeling off raw silk from a cocoon. The movements, like clouds floating in the sky, are spry and light, but well-balanced and steady. Motion is even and fluid, the muscles neither stiff nor rigid. Breathing should be deep and even. . . the mind is tranquil but alert, with consciousness commanding the body. In practising T'ai Chi Chuan it is essential that movements be guided by consciousness and that there be stillness in movement – a unity of stillness and motion."

Throughout the form all parts of the body should be relaxed yet alert. Eye movements are focused, not dreamy; hands are relaxed, fingers naturally curved (unless directed to take other particular shapes). All movements should be made smoothly and come from the Tan Tien (p.24) in the lower abdomen, your centre of gravity. Breathing should be deep and even. Your tongue should remain touching the roof of your mouth throughout the form.

To perform the 24-step form you will need a clear area about 17 feet (5 m) square. In China people practise outside under trees in the early morning. Most students try to learn one or two steps at a time, letting each step sink into the mind before proceeding to the next one. In Chinese tradition, you learn to direct the movements to the "Four Corners" of the earth, the North, South, East and West. In time you will be able to perform the steps without breaking the flow. The form usually takes 5 minutes, but from time to time it is a good idea to vary the pace – do it faster and more vigorously on occasion, and more slowly than normal once in a while.

Step 1 Heaven and Earth

This is the classic opening step, symbolizing Man's coming from the Earth and aspiring to Heaven. You can practise this step as a Taoist breathing exercise in its own right, performing the movement slowly and continuously, with deep and slow breathing – inhaling as the arms rise, exhaling as they sink down.

1a *Stand upright with your chest relaxed, arms by your sides. Your feet should be less than shoulders' width apart. The tip of your tongue should touch the roof of your mouth (the tongue is a link in the Taoist circle of energy), and it should stay like this throughout the form. Breathe evenly through your nose from the Tan Tien (p.24). Look forward and slightly downward. Hold this posture for a few moments before moving.*

1a

1b *Breathing in, raise both your arms to shoulder height straight to the front, palms downward. Let them float upward slowly like gentle waves. Try to feel that you are moving through the air – it helps to imagine a slight resistance to the movement.*

1b

1c *As you breathe out, lower your body by gently bending your knees until they are above your toes, but no further. At the same time, lower your arms to waist height, until your hands are horizontal. This movement opens your energy channels. You may be able to sense the Chi in a slight tingling in the fingertips.*

1c

Step 2 Part the Wild Horse's Mane to Both Sides

This epitomizes the concept of harmonizing opposites: a movement of precision and calm is made in a moment of turmoil – when handling a wild horse. Try to feel that you are doing what the title suggests. This step is also used as a drill for training, returning to 2a from 2k, repeated as often as you wish. Look forward, or at the hand that is highest, as you complete each move.

2a

2a *From 1c, shift slightly to the right, transferring your weight onto your right leg. Bring the ball of your left foot to rest beside the right, heel off the ground. Bring your right hand to chest height, palm down, and circle your left hand until its palm faces upward, directly under the right palm. Imagine you are holding a beach ball. This is called the "hold ball" gesture, and recurs many times in the Short Form. Rest your eyes on your right hand.*

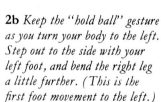

2b *Keep the "hold ball" gesture as you turn your body to the left. Step out to the side with your left foot, and bend the right leg a little further. (This is the first foot movement to the left.)*

2b

2c

2c *Move your weight forward onto your left leg. Lift the left arm across to shoulder height, palm up, and lower the right hand to waist height, palm down. Look at your left hand.*

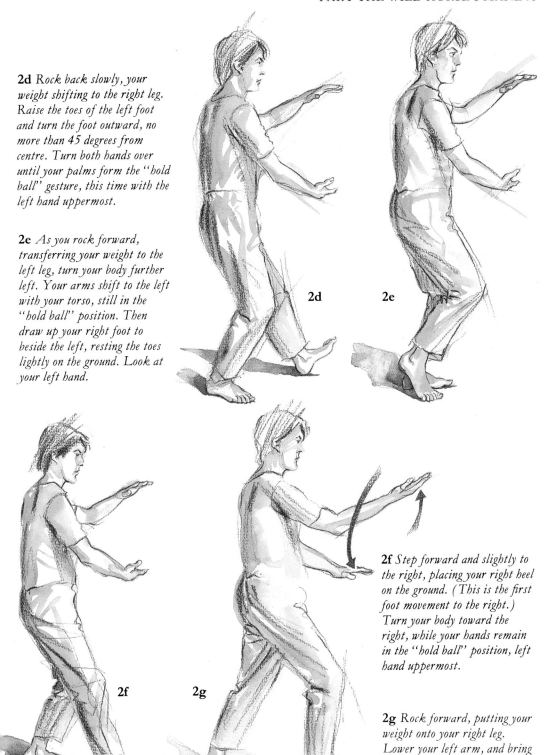

2d *Rock back slowly, your weight shifting to the right leg. Raise the toes of the left foot and turn the foot outward, no more than 45 degrees from centre. Turn both hands over until your palms form the "hold ball" gesture, this time with the left hand uppermost.*

2e *As you rock forward, transferring your weight to the left leg, turn your body further left. Your arms shift to the left with your torso, still in the "hold ball" position. Then draw up your right foot to beside the left, resting the toes lightly on the ground. Look at your left hand.*

2d

2e

2f

2g

2f *Step forward and slightly to the right, placing your right heel on the ground. (This is the first foot movement to the right.) Turn your body toward the right, while your hands remain in the "hold ball" position, left hand uppermost.*

2g *Rock forward, putting your weight onto your right leg. Lower your left arm, and bring your right arm upward, palm facing up. Rest your eyes on your right hand.*

2h *Rock back slightly, placing your weight on your left leg, and rotating the right foot outward on the heel. Turn your hands over, right hand uppermost, palm down, left hand beneath in the "hold ball" position.*

2i *Rock forward onto your right foot, and turn slightly to the right, and keeping the "hold ball" position, right hand uppermost. Draw your left foot up beside the right foot, toes resting on the ground.*

2h

2i

2j

2k

2j *Step to the left, placing your left heel on the ground. (See also photograph on facing page.)*

2k *Shift your weight onto your left leg, pivoting the ball of the right foot outward. Bring your left arm up to shoulder height, palm up. Lower the right hand, palm down. (2j and k repeat 2b and c.)*

Position j (and b) from Step 2, Part the Wild Horse's Mane.

Step 3 White Crane Spreads its Wings

The white crane is a symbol of longevity in Chinese culture; it is often depicted with pine trees and mushrooms, which also symbolize long life. This movement enables your breath to expand from your Tan Tien (p.24). Look straight ahead of you while performing this step.

3a *Step up from behind and transfer your weight to your right leg. Your arms make the "hold ball" gesture (2a, p.92), left hand uppermost, to the front of your body.*

3a

3b *Slide your left leg forward on the ball of the foot. (This is known as the "empty step" since it bears no real weight.) Cross your arms to bring your left hand down, palm downward, and your right hand upward to head level, with the palm toward your face. Look straight ahead.*

3b

Step 4 Brush Knee and Twist Hip on Both Sides

The movement of the elbow with the knee, the shoulder with the hip, and the wrist with the ankle is co-ordinated in a smooth linkage – referred to, in the modern Chinese manual to the Short Form, as "reeling silk from a cocoon". The use of the waist in this step massages the internal organs, invigorating them and toning the surrounding musculature and ligaments.

4a *Turn your body a little further to the left. Circle your right hand downward, palm up, and at the same time move your left hand upward, palm toward the right, to shoulder height. Glance at the left hand.*

4a

4b (4i) *Continue to circle your arms, bringing your right arm up, partly extended, to face level, palm toward the left, while your left hand sinks downward toward the left hip, palm down. Place your left leg further forward, with the heel on the ground.*

4b

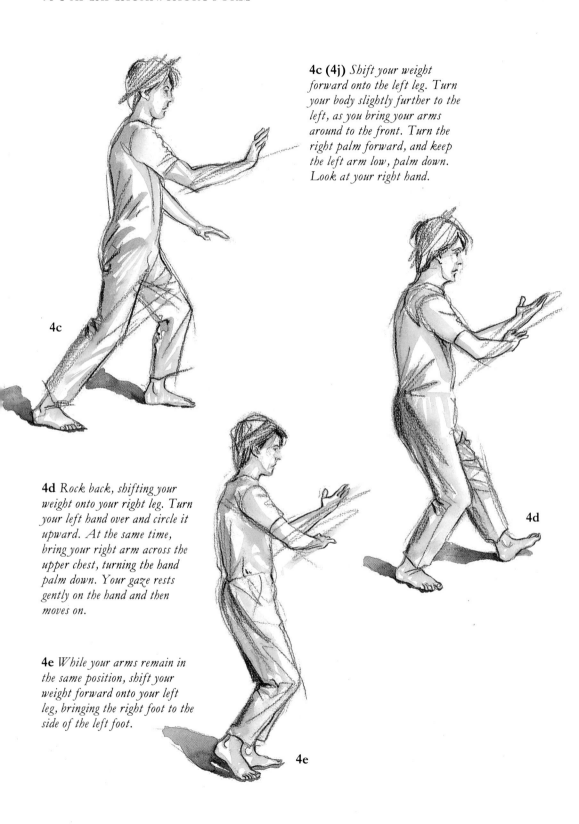

4c (4j) *Shift your weight forward onto the left leg. Turn your body slightly further to the left, as you bring your arms around to the front. Turn the right palm forward, and keep the left arm low, palm down. Look at your right hand.*

4c

4d

4d *Rock back, shifting your weight onto your right leg. Turn your left hand over and circle it upward. At the same time, bring your right arm across the upper chest, turning the hand palm down. Your gaze rests gently on the hand and then moves on.*

4e *While your arms remain in the same position, shift your weight forward onto your left leg, bringing the right foot to the side of the left foot.*

4e

4f *Circle your arms, and bring your left hand up toward face level, palm toward the right, while your right arm sinks down toward the right hip, palm down. Step forward with your right leg, placing the heel only on the ground.*

4f

4g

4g *Now shift your weight forward and turn your body slightly to the right, keeping an upright posture. Turn your left wrist so that the palm faces forward. Keep the right hand low, palm down.*

4h *Rock back, shifting your weight onto your left leg. Leaving your right heel on the ground, pivot the right foot to the right, and turn your body in the same direction. Turn your right hand over, and circle it upward while you bring your left hand downward across your chest, palm downward.*

4h

To continue
4i and j *Repeat 4b and c.*

Step 5 Hand Strums the Lute

This step is characterized by the distinctive position of the hands, held together in front of the body. It is similar to the classical position of the musicians' hands in Chinese opera, and is often referred to as "Playing the Pipa"(the Chinese guitar).

5a *Bring your right foot up to your left foot and transfer your weight onto it. Your legs remain bent at the knee, your right foot turned slightly outward. Your arms remain in the same position as 4c, the left hand at hip level, palm down, the right hand raised, and palm forward.*

5a

5b *Slide the front foot forward, keeping most of the weight on the back leg. Bring your left arm up and to the front, palm toward the right, and bring your right hand to the centre line of your body, palm toward the left. Look at your left hand.*

5b

Step 6 Repulse the Monkey

Intelligent, mischievous, famed for its dexterity, the monkey is much respected in China. (It is one of the Twelve Animals in Hsing I, p.60.) While you perform this step your head and neck should be aligned with your torso – in other words, your nose should remain in line with your navel.

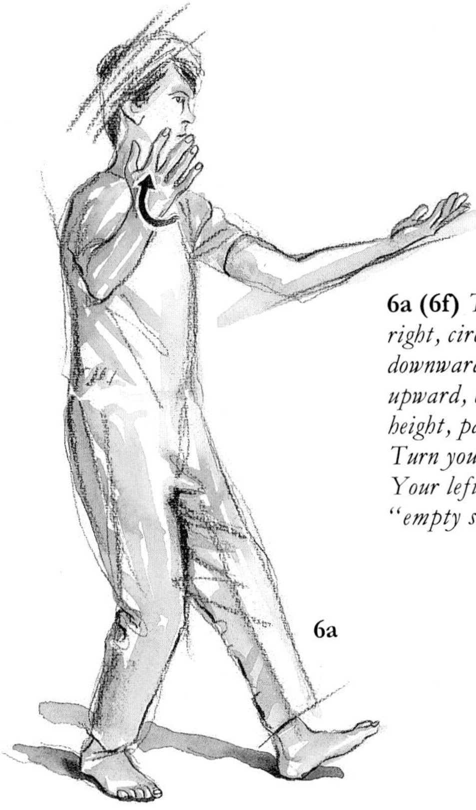

6a (6f) *Turn slightly to the right, circling your right hand downward, outward and upward, bringing it to shoulder height, palm toward the left. Turn your left palm upward. Your left leg remains in an "empty step" (3b, p.96).*

6a

6b (6g) *Step backward with your left leg, stepping first onto the ball of your left foot, and then transferring your weight to it. Draw your left arm back, elbow bent, to waist height, the hand palm upward, at the same time pushing forward with the right arm, palm forward at shoulder height.*

6b

6c (6h) *Raise the ball of your right foot in an "empty step" (3b, p.96). Circle the left arm downward, then up to shoulder height, palm upward. Turn your right hand over, so that both palms face upward.*

6c

6d

6d (6i) *Bring your right leg back, close to the left ankle, keeping your weight on your left leg. At the same time, lower your right arm, bending the elbow to bring it backward at waist height.*

6e (6j) *Continue to draw your right leg back behind you, then transfer your weight to it. Your left arm circles upward and down, then pushes outward, palm forward.*

To continue
6f, g, h, i, j *Repeat the actions of 6a-e.*

6e

Moving forward from position f, Step 7, Grasp the Bird's Tail, Left Side.

Step 7 Grasp the Bird's Tail, Left Side

"Grasp the Sparrow's Tail While Warding Off the Tiger" is another title for this step, referring to the role of opposites (p.84), and the balance of Yin and Yang within the movement. It is one of the oldest sequences in T'ai Chi and it comprises four basic moves – ward off, roll back, press, and push – which recur in both Basic Powers and in Pushing Hands (pp.140-6). Look at your upper hand after each of the movements shown below.

7a

7a Draw your left foot back to the right foot, leaving only the ball of the foot on the ground. Bring your left hand downward and across your body at waist level, palm upward, while your right arm circles outward, up and then over, palm down. This brings you to the "hold ball" position (2a, p.92), with the right hand uppermost. Look at your right hand.

7b

7b Step out with your left leg forward and slightly to the side, heel to the ground.

7c Shifting your weight to your left leg, cross your arms in front of your body, raising your left forearm to slightly below shoulder height, palm facing your right shoulder. At the same time, lower your right arm to waist height, palm down.

7c

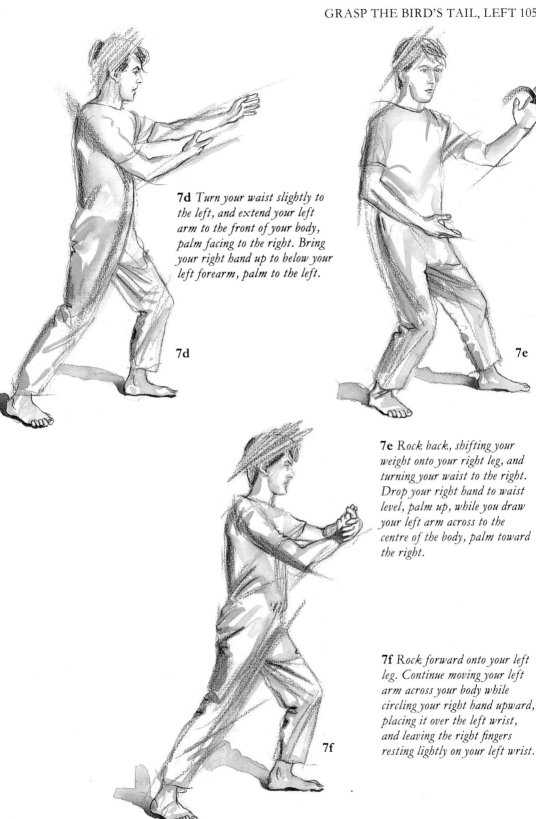

7d *Turn your waist slightly to the left, and extend your left arm to the front of your body, palm facing to the right. Bring your right hand up to below your left forearm, palm to the left.*

7d

7e

7e *Rock back, shifting your weight onto your right leg, and turning your waist to the right. Drop your right hand to waist level, palm up, while you draw your left arm across to the centre of the body, palm toward the right.*

7f

7f *Rock forward onto your left leg. Continue moving your left arm across your body while circling your right hand upward, placing it over the left wrist, and leaving the right fingers resting lightly on your left wrist.*

7g *Shifting your weight onto your left leg, press both hands forward and together. Your right hand should slide over your left, so that both arms extend forward, shoulders' width apart, hands palm down.*

7g

7h *Rock your weight back onto your right leg, and lift the ball of the left foot. Draw your wrists down to waist level, and circle the palms of the hands forward and up.*

7i *Rock forward, shifting your weight onto the left leg again. Push your arms forward at chest height, palms to the front.*

7h

7i

Step 8 Grasp the Bird's Tail, Right Side

The movements of Step 8 repeat 7a to 7i but on the right side of the body. The steps are said to be good for those suffering from gastro-intestinal disorders or diabetes, since they benefit certain internal organs. While performing this step you should look ahead of you and at your left hand, keeping your nose in line with your navel.

8 Transitional Move

Rock your weight back onto your right foot, raising the toes of the left foot and turning them inward, then lowering them to the ground. Raise both hands a little further, to shoulder height, palms forward, and bring your right hand across the body. (This takes you back to the start of Step 7, except that Step 8 is performed on the other side of the body.)

8

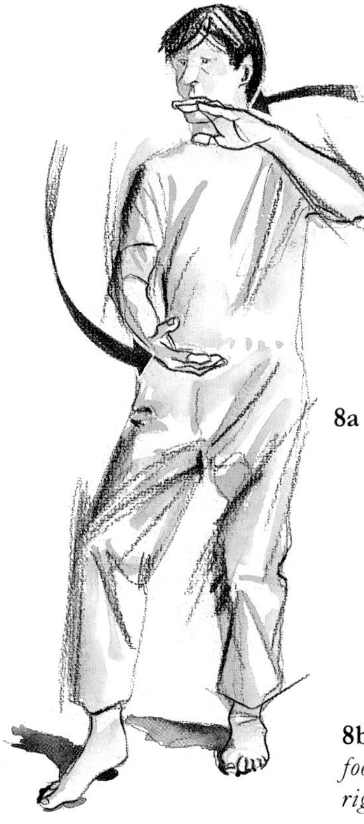

8a *Transfer your weight to your left leg, slightly raising your right heel. Continue the right arm's circle around, down, and to waist level, palm up. At the same time bring your left arm across the body to the "hold ball" position, left hand uppermost.*

8a

8b

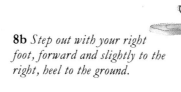

8b *Step out with your right foot, forward and slightly to the right, heel to the ground.*

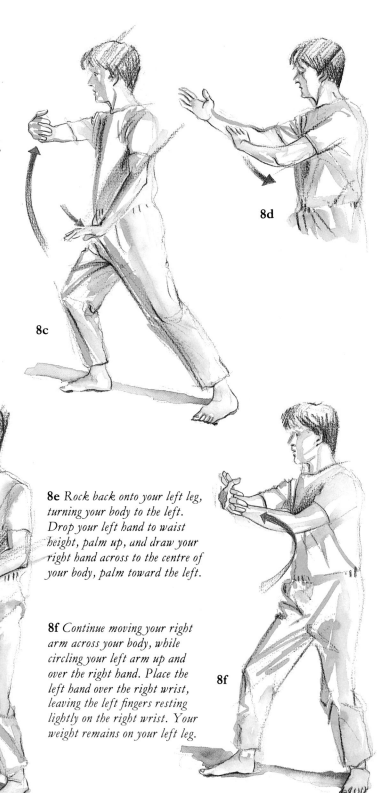

8c *Shift your weight onto the right foot. Then cross your arms, so that your right hand is raised almost to shoulder height, palm inward, and your left arm is lowered to waist level, with the palm down.*

8d *Turn your body slightly further to the right, and extend your right arm to the front, palm toward the left. Bring your left hand up to below your right forearm, palm facing up and to the right.*

8e *Rock back onto your left leg, turning your body to the left. Drop your left hand to waist height, palm up, and draw your right hand across to the centre of your body, palm toward the left.*

8f *Continue moving your right arm across your body, while circling your left arm up and over the right hand. Place the left hand over the right wrist, leaving the left fingers resting lightly on the right wrist. Your weight remains on your left leg.*

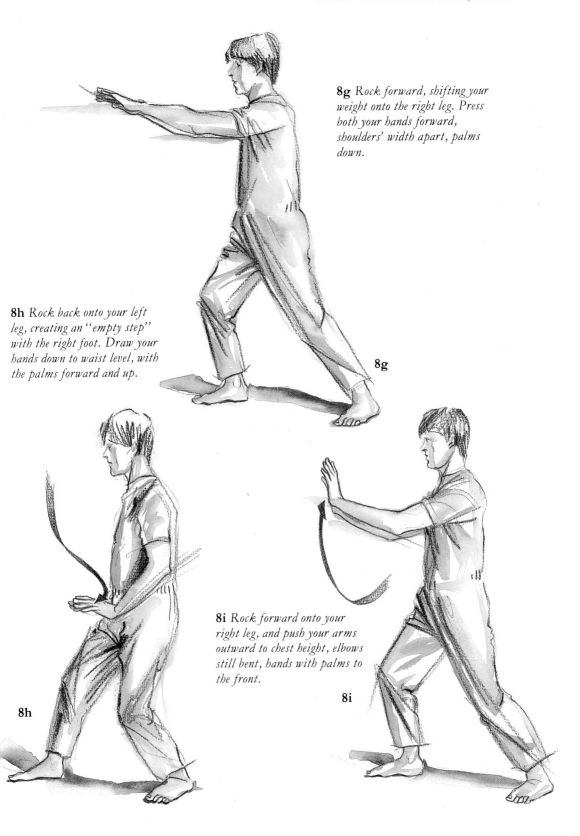

8g *Rock forward, shifting your weight onto the right leg. Press both your hands forward, shoulders' width apart, palms down.*

8h *Rock back onto your left leg, creating an "empty step" with the right foot. Draw your hands down to waist level, with the palms forward and up.*

8g

8i *Rock forward onto your right leg, and push your arms outward to chest height, elbows still bent, hands with palms to the front.*

8i

8h

Step 9 Single Whip 1

In this step, Chi, or vital energy (p.24) flows through to your fingertips, in the same way that the tip of a whip in a whiplash reaction releases the greatest energy.

9a *Rock your weight back onto your left foot, raise the toes of the right foot, and turn them inward, then return them to the ground. Your body turns slightly toward the left. Circle your left arm upward, palm down, and your right arm downward, palm up, so that you arrive at the "hold ball" position, left hand uppermost.*

9a

9b (11a) *Shift your weight to the right leg, making an "empty step" with your left foot, toes just touching the ground. (In 9b this movement completes your turn, so that you face the way you came.) At the same time, bring your right hand across your body at face height. Look at your right palm.*

9b

Hand position for 9c-e

9c

9c (11b) *Extend the right arm to the side and turn your right hand over. Drop the wrist, holding your thumb and first three fingers lightly together (as in the close-up above, far left). This is the Single Whip gesture. Turn your left forearm so that the palm of the hand is toward you. Your legs remain in the same position, the left foot on its toes, your weight resting on the right leg.*

9d (11c) *Step forward with the left heel and begin to shift your weight onto the left leg. Look at your left hand.*

9e (11d) *Stretch your right leg while you rock your weight forward onto your left leg, putting the whole foot down. At the same time turn your left hand over so that your palm faces forward. Your right hand remains in the Single Whip position. (The photograph on p.82 shows 9d moving into 9e.)*

9d

9e

Step 10 Wave Hands Like Clouds

The repeated billowing movements of your hands represent the interaction of opposites – the clouds (the substantial) generating thunder and lightning (the insubstantial). This exercise encourages a more healthy posture and massages the internal organs. It is also recommended for both respiratory and circulatory problems. Let your eyes briefly follow your hands as they pass your face.

10a *Shift your weight to the right leg, then turn your left foot inward, so that your body twists to the right. Open the right hand, palm outward, then circle your left arm down and across your body so that the palm faces upward.*

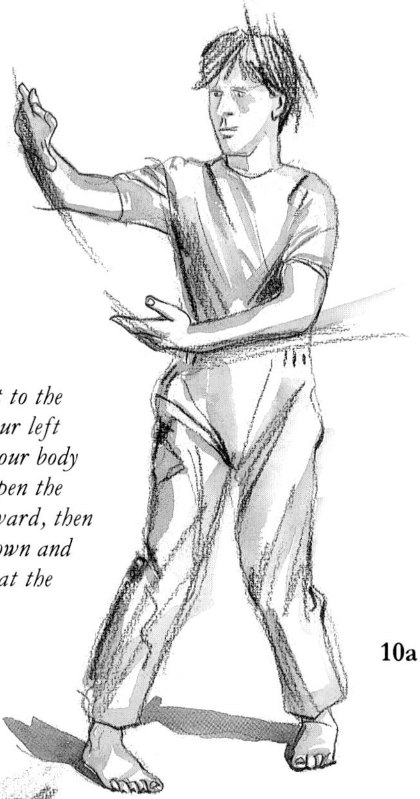

10a

10b

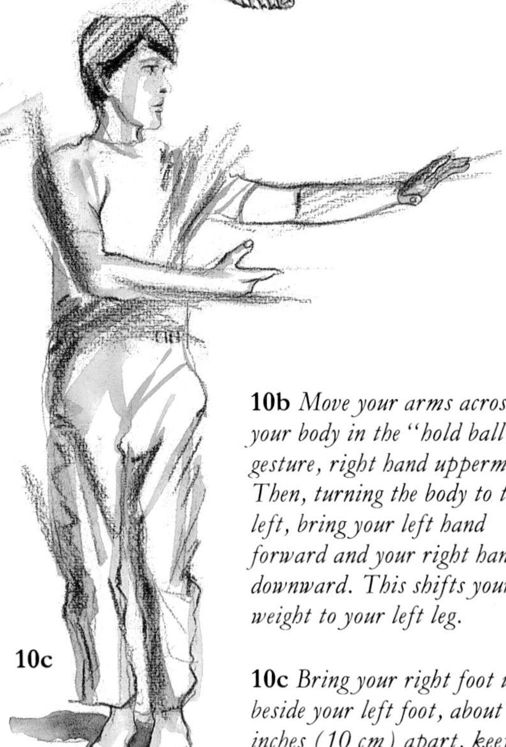

10c

10b *Move your arms across your body in the "hold ball" gesture, right hand uppermost. Then, turning the body to the left, bring your left hand forward and your right hand downward. This shifts your weight to your left leg.*

10c *Bring your right foot up beside your left foot, about 4 inches (10 cm) apart, keeping the knees bent.*

Position e from Step 13, Kick with Right Heel.

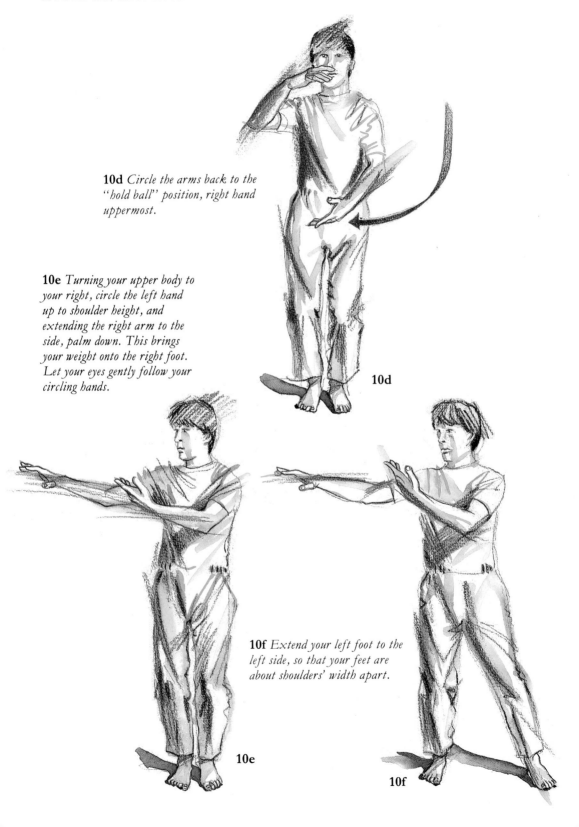

10d *Circle the arms back to the "hold ball" position, right hand uppermost.*

10e *Turning your upper body to your right, circle the left hand up to shoulder height, and extending the right arm to the side, palm down. This brings your weight onto the right foot. Let your eyes gently follow your circling hands.*

10f *Extend your left foot to the left side, so that your feet are about shoulders' width apart.*

10d

10e

10f

10g *Circle your arms across your body, raising your left arm and letting the right arm sink into the "hold ball" position, left hand uppermost. This brings your weight onto both your legs.*

10g

10h *Extend both your arms to your left, the left arm straight, the right arm across the body at chest height. Transfer your weight onto your left leg.*

10h

10i *Bring your right leg in to beside your left leg, about 4 inches (10 cm) apart. Begin to circle your left arm downward and your right arm upward toward the "hold ball" position, right hand uppermost.*

10i

To continue
10j, k, l, m, n, o *Repeat the movements of 10d-i.*

Step 11 Single Whip 2
Step 11 repeats the first Single Whip sequence on the same side of the body.

To continue
11a, b, c, d *Repeat the movements of 9b-e (pp.110-11).*

Step 12 High Pat on Horse

This title comes from the high position of the right hand in position b. The movement is much practised by T'ai Chi students to improve balance and give added strength to the body and the legs.

12a *Feet together, turn both hands so that the palms face upward. Transfer your weight to the right leg.*

12a

12b *Slide your left foot forward into an "empty step", with the ball of the foot on the ground. Bring the left hand back and down to waist height, palm up, and push the right hand forward at eye level and slightly upward, with the palm facing down. Your eyes should rest on your right hand.*

12b

Step 13 Kick with Right Heel

This technique involves a higher degree of balance than most other steps in the Short Form. It co-ordinates the separating of the hands and a kicking action that stretches the tendons of the heels – and it is sometimes known as "Stretching the Heel".

13a

13a *Move your left foot forward and put your heel on the ground, toes pointing to the left and outward. Bring your left hand up to inside the right wrist, palm facing inward.*

13b

13b *Rock forward, shifting your weight onto your left foot. Separate your arms so that they are parallel and both the palms of the hands face forward.*

13c

13c *Circle both arms downward while you start to lift your right foot, raising the heel first, and bringing it up to beside the left foot. Cross the hands at the wrist, with the left hand inside, and both palms facing inward.*

13d *Raise both hands together to face height, palms inward, keeping your legs in the same position, your weight resting on your left foot, the right foot beside it but lightly resting on the toes.*

13d

13e *Separate your arms and turn both hands to the front palms forward. Now kick out to the right with the right foot, pushing your heel forward and to the right, about 45 degrees outward from the centre line of the body. Look at your right hand. (See also photograph, p.113.)*

13e

Step 14 Twin Dragon Searches for the Pearl

This step is sometimes called "Dragon Embracing the Moon", describing the twin action of the arms and hands. It also has a more combative title: "Strike Opponent's Ears with Both Fists".

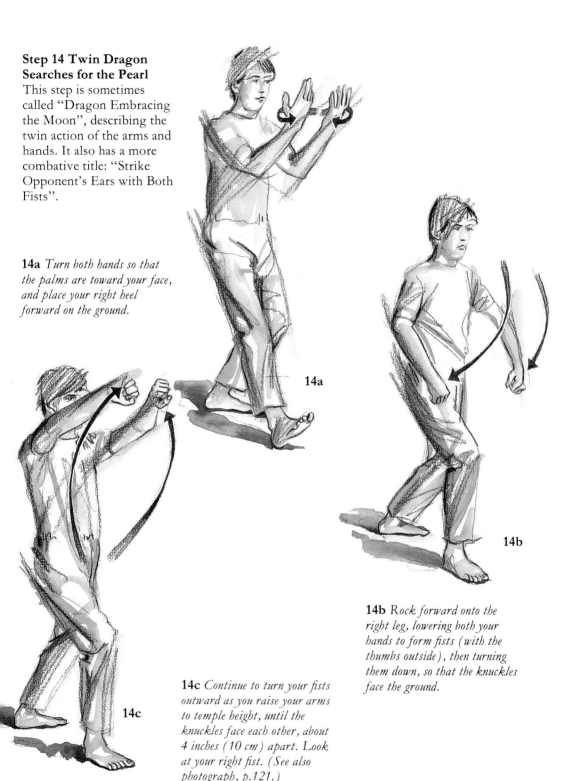

14a *Turn both hands so that the palms are toward your face, and place your right heel forward on the ground.*

14a

14b

14c

14b *Rock forward onto the right leg, lowering both your hands to form fists (with the thumbs outside), then turning them down, so that the knuckles face the ground.*

14c *Continue to turn your fists outward as you raise your arms to temple height, until the knuckles face each other, about 4 inches (10 cm) apart. Look at your right fist. (See also photograph, p.121.)*

Step 15 Turn and Kick with Left Heel

This repeats the kicking exercise of Step 13, but with the left leg. Notice that the T'ai Chi kick is delivered with the heel. You should try to pull the front of your foot up and back when your leg is fully extended, in position 15f on page 122.

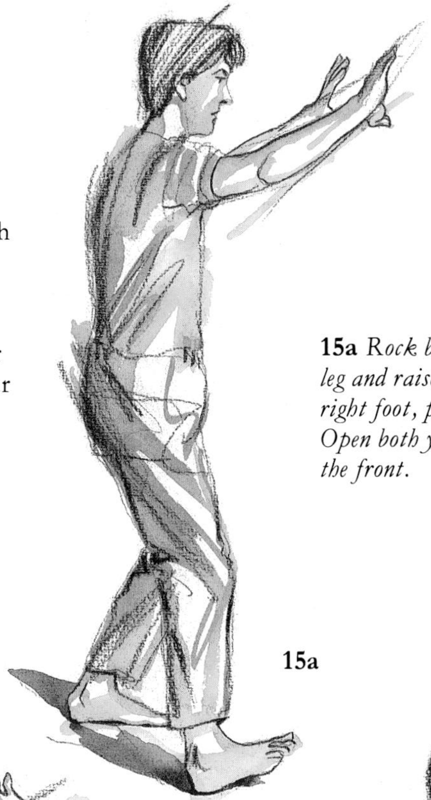

15a *Rock back onto your left leg and raise the toes of your right foot, pivoting it inward. Open both your hands toward the front.*

15a

15b *Drop the toes of the right foot to the ground. Turn your body to the left and begin to circle both your arms outward. Look at your left hand.*

15c *Keep turning your body to the left, transferring your weight onto the right foot, making an "empty step" with your left leg, toes to the ground. At the same time, circle both hands downward, so that the palms face down.*

15b

15c

Boxing ears position from Step 14, Twin Dragon Searches for the Pearl.

15d *Continue to circle both arms, upward and together, the right wrist crossing inside the left as they reach chest height (as in the close-up below). Look forward and to the left.*

15d

15e

Hand positions for 15d

15e *Bending your knee, raise your left foot to knee height. Your hands remain crossed as in position 15d.*

15f

15f *Kick to the left with the left foot, pushing the heel forward while you separate your hands, palms forward.*

16a *Bring the left foot back to your right foot, and make the Single Whip gesture with your right hand (p.111). At the same time, bring your left hand across the body at chest height, palm to the right.*

16a

Step 16 Snake Creeps Down, Left Side

One of the Twelve Animals in Hsing I (p.60), the snake is reputed to be the legless body of a dragon. The title of this step reflects the desire to draw energy from the Earth, and a willingness to embrace this element. Try to imagine yourself moving like the snake as it glides over the Earth. This is also called "Push Down and Stand on One Leg".

16b

16b *Turn to face the right and slide your left leg back, heel first, keeping the leg straight. Your right leg should bend at the knee. Reach forward with your right arm, the hand still in Single Whip, while you lower your left arm to waist level.*

16c *Twist your left foot to point slightly outward. Circle your left arm and lower your torso so that the left arm is parallel to the leg. Meanwhile take your right arm back, and turn your hand over so that the fingers, still in Single Whip form, point up and back. (The photograph on p.129 shows 16c from the other side.)*

16d *Stretch your right leg as you shift your weight forward, rotating the right foot on the ball to point inward at about 45 degrees. Raise your left hand to chest height, palm facing forward. Leave your right hand in Single Whip gesture, fingers pointing upward. (On p.135 the photograph shows 16d from the other side.)*

16e *Bring your right knee forward and up to waist height, and lower your left hand to the same level, palm down. Circle your right hand forward and up so that the palm faces to the left. Look at your right hand.*

Step 17 Snake Creeps Down, Right Side
This movement repeats Step 16, but on the right side of the body. Try to feel yourself moving fluidly down, across, and upward, proceeding smoothly into the next position.

17a *Bring your right foot down beside your left foot, turning your body 90 degrees to your left. Circle the right hand over and across your chest, palm facing left, while your left hand circles up to shoulder height to the Single Whip hand position. Look in the direction of your left hand.*

17a

17b

17b *Bend your left knee as you slide your right leg back and to the side, heel first, keeping the leg straight. Lean forward, bringing your right arm parallel to your right leg. Your left arm extends behind you, with the fingers pointing up.*

17c *Twist your right foot so that it points slightly outward. Bend the right knee and keep your torso low as you move it to the right, circling your right arm to align with your leg.*

17c

17d *Shift your weight onto your right leg, and turn your body further to the right. Rotate your left foot on the ball so it points forward. Raise your right arm to chest height, palm forward. The left arm remains in Single Whip position with the fingers pointing upward and backward.*

17d

17e *Now bring your left knee forward and up to hip height while you lower your right hand to the same level, palm facing downward. Circle your left arm forward and up toward face height, turning your hand so that the palm faces right.*

17e

Step 18 Old Lady Works the Shuttles to Both Sides

The hands and waist work here in a manner that imitates the actions of weaving. In some of the T'ai Chi Long Forms this step is known as the "Four Corners", since it was performed to the North, South, East, and West.

18a *Lower your left foot and step forward, heel to the ground. Turn the foot outward a little. Your left arm circles upward, with the palm facing down, the right arm sinks down, until you reach "hold ball" position, left hand uppermost.*

18a

18b *Rock your weight forward onto your left foot, circling the right arm up and to the front, moving the palm up toward your face. Lower your left arm across your chest, palm down.*

18b

18c

18c *Step about 45 degrees to the right with the right foot, heel to the ground. Let your arms stay in the same position.*

18d *Shift your weight to the right foot, and lower the toes to the ground. Turn your body to the right while you twist your right hand outward, palm outward. Push your left hand forward and to the right. Look at your left hand.*

18d

18e *Rock back onto your left foot, leaving your right foot on the ground, toes raised. Circle your arms, continuing to raise the right hand and lower the left into the "hold ball" position, right hand uppermost.*

18e

Moving from position b to c in Step 16, Snake Creeps Down, Left Side.

18f *Now rock forward onto your right foot, circling the left hand up and to the front, palm toward your face. Lower your right arm across your chest.*

18f

18g

18g *Step about 45 degrees to the left with your left foot, heel to the ground. Your arms stay in the same position.*

18h

18h *Shift your weight forward onto the left foot. Turn your body to the left and twist your left hand so that the palm faces outward. Push your right hand forward, and look between your hands.*

Step 19 Pluck Needle from the Sea Bottom
The descending energy in this step is used to reach downward and place the right hand precisely on the target. Imagine that your right hand is plucking the needle from the sea bed while your left hand represents the rippling surface of the sea.

19a

19a *Bring your right foot up beside your left foot while you turn your body to the right. Your left arm begins to circle to the left and down.*

19b *Transfer your weight to the right leg as you circle your left arm to the left and down to waist level. At the same time, raise your right hand to face level, palm facing inward.*

19b

19c *Slide your left foot forward on the toes, in an "empty step" posture. Bring your right hand down, fingers pointing to the ground. This is "plucking the needle". Look at the ground ahead. Your left hand stays at waist level, palm down.*

19c

Step 20 Flash the Arm

This step is also known as "Separating the Hands". The posture mimics the action of drawing a bow.

20a *Take a step forward with the heel of your left foot. Raise your right arm to about chest height, palm inward, fingers pointing down, then raise your left arm, placing the palm of the hand inside the right elbow.*

20b *Rock forward onto the left foot. Your arms remain in the same position.*

20c *Push your left hand forward, palm to the front, and draw your right hand back past your temple, palm facing outward. This gesture imitates the action of an archer drawing a bow. Your legs stay in the same position. Look at your outstretched left hand.*

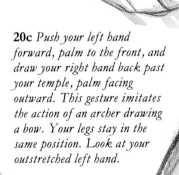

20a

20b

20c

Step 21 Turn, Deflect, Parry, and Punch
These movements contain a series of defensive and offensive actions which call for a high degree of co-ordination. The step starts with a turn and proceeds to the forward drive to punch.

21a *Rock backward onto your right leg and twist your left foot inward. Bring your left hand across the body at head height, as if to parry a blow, and make a fist, thumb outside, palm facing outward. Your right hand remains at shoulder height, palm facing outward.*

21a

21b *Shift your weight to the left foot and twist your body to the left. Now bring your right arm across the body and downward, making a second fist, thumb outside, palm down. Your left hand remains at head height, palm outward.*

21c *Rotate your body to the right, making an "empty step" forward with the right foot, heel up. Bring your left hand across your body. Your right hand remains in a fist.*

21b

21c

21d *Bring the right foot into the "kick step" position – pulling the foot back a little, raising the heel a little further. Begin to raise your right fist inside the left arm, and lower your left hand, palm down.*

21e *Kick forward with your right foot, heel first, and rotate your right arm so that the fist faces up, and look at your right fist.*

21d

21e

21f *Place your right foot down and to the front, pointing about 45 degrees outward from the centre of your body.*

21f

Position d from Step 16, Snake Creeps Down, Left Side.

21g *Step forward with your left foot, leaving your weight on the right leg. Rotate your left hand so that the palm faces toward your right, about waist level. Your right arm remains to the front at about waist height, with the hand in an upward-turned fist.*

21g

21h *Now rock forward, transferring your weight to your left leg. At the same time, punch with your right fist, forward and to the centre, the palm of the fist facing to the left. Your left arm remains outstretched, above waist level. Look forward.*

21h

Step 22 Apparent Close Up

This step is a direct application of one of T'ai Chi's guiding principles – you make an "apparent" movement that conceals your real intention. Another example is when you make yourself appear substantial or insubstantial to deceive your opponent, presenting a false target to him or her.

22a *Place your left hand under your right forearm, lightly holding the arm, then begin to slide it forward. The right hand begins to open, palm up.*

22a

22b *Separate the hands, and open them both, palms forward and down. Then rock backward onto your right leg, bringing both hands downward to the Tan Tien, keeping your palms forward and down.*

22c *Rock forward again onto your left foot, pushing to the front with both hands at chest height, palms facing forward. Look ahead.*

22b

22c

Step 23 Cross Hands

This is a final gathering of vital energy. As in Pa Kua (pp.64-81), the arms trace the circle of the Universe, and then divide it into Yin and Yang.

23a *Rock backward onto your right foot and twist your left foot inward, turning your body to the right. Circle your arms outward at shoulder height, palms outward. Look at your right hand.*

23b *Shift your weight onto your left leg, leaving both feet in the same position. Continue to circle your arms outward and down, with your hands palms down. You are reaching out and drawing energy into the centre of your body.*

23c *Draw your right foot back, keeping the feet about shoulders' width apart. Your weight is equally distributed. Move both your arms downward and inward, turning the palms upward, and crossing your hands, with the left hand on the inside. Finally, raise your crossed hands up to chest height, palms inward.*

Step 24 Closing Form
The last step is the exact reverse of the opening step (p.91), and signifies a return from Heaven to Earth, and the benefits that are brought back from Heaven. You should exhale with the downward movement of your arms.

24a *Push your crossed hands forward at shoulder height, turning your right hand over, palm down, and sliding your left palm over your right hand. Your feet remain shoulders' width apart.*

24a

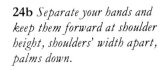

24b

24b *Separate your hands and keep them forward at shoulder height, shoulders' width apart, palms down.*

24c

24c *Lower the arms to the front of your body, palms down. Look forward. Then relax your wrists so that both hands drop downward. Straighten your legs. Finally, conclude the form by bringing the left foot close beside the right foot.*

The Basic Powers

Up to this point the T'ai Chi postures have appeared primarily as exercises for good health – but it must not be forgotten that the art has other aims. The Basic Powers or Forces shown here have been selected from a number of defensive techniques which are usually practised by students after their Short Form session. They involve deflecting and repulsing an attacker rather than initiating an attack – in fact, the defender uses the attacker's momentum instead of relying on his or her own strength (see also Yielding, rootedness, and expulsion, pp.84-5).

If you are attacked, you should try to bear in mind two general rules; the first is to avoid conflict if at all possible; the second is that if it's reasonable to run for it, do so, rather than standing and fighting. Only when there is no other option should you apply your T'ai Chi. **Caution** Beginners should not practise these techniques without a trained martial arts' teacher's supervision.

NB To help differentiate the partners, the defender is labelled A, the attacker is B.

Shoulder Strike
The defender thwarts an attack to the neck from behind. This must be done quickly and smoothly.

1a *B approaches A from behind and grabs A around the neck. A takes a large step back, placing his or her right foot between B's legs, keeping the heel up. A grasps B's right hand with his or her right hand.*

1b *A rocks backward onto his or her right leg, and moves upward abruptly, opening both arms, throwing B's hands and arms outward, at the same time using the shoulders to "bounce" B backward.*

B   A

A   B

1a   1b

Roll Back
The defender deflects a
"one-sided" frontal attack –
usually a punch to the face.

2a *B aims a right-handed blow
toward A's face. A dodges to
the side, takes a rooted stance –
legs about 2 feet (60 cm) apart,
knees slightly bent – and catches
B's right arm, with the right
hand over B's wrist and the left
hand on the back of B's elbow.*

2b *A shifts weight onto the
right foot and with the right
hand pulls B forward and down
in the direction of the punch,
levering B's elbow down with the
left hand on the joint.*

2c *A twists to the right and
shifts his or her weight forward,
continuing to pull B forward
and down. (This move can end
with B pinned to the ground and
immobilized by pressure against
the elbow joint.)*

Push Out

This is a defence against a frontal attack with both hands to the neck. A's speed and force should build up steadily from start to finish.

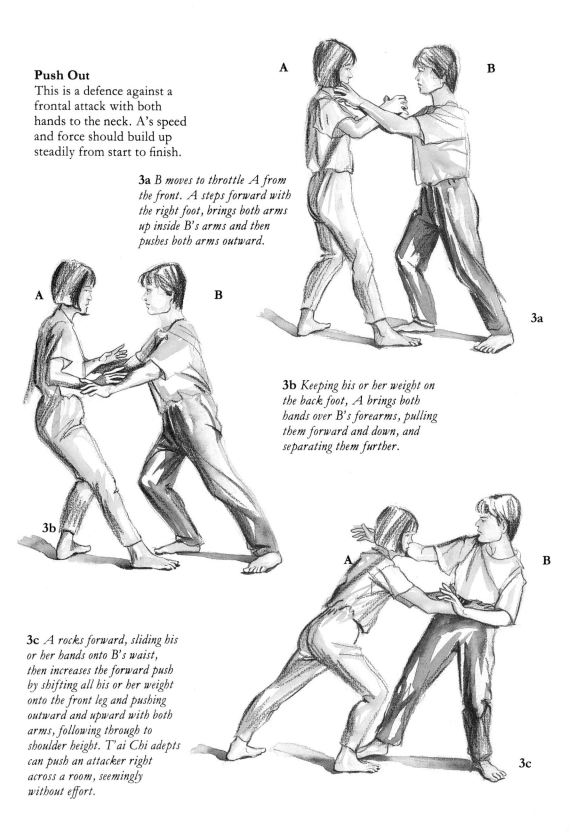

3a *B moves to throttle A from the front. A steps forward with the right foot, brings both arms up inside B's arms and then pushes both arms outward.*

3a

3b *Keeping his or her weight on the back foot, A brings both hands over B's forearms, pulling them forward and down, and separating them further.*

3b

3c *A rocks forward, sliding his or her hands onto B's waist, then increases the forward push by shifting all his or her weight onto the front leg and pushing outward and upward with both arms, following through to shoulder height. T'ai Chi adepts can push an attacker right across a room, seemingly without effort.*

3c

Position 1b, Shoulder strike.

Pushing Hands

T'ai Chi self defence requires excellent balance and fine timing. Pushing Hands was devised to develop these skills. It is practised as a rhythmical, non-competitive exercise in which you are in constant contact with your partner. Ideally, you should practise with someone of about your own weight and size.

While practising Pushing Hands, try to feel your partner's state of balance, and even his or her mental state. If you want to you can close your eyes, but make sure you are alert at all times. As you gain experience you will find it easier to detect the moment when your partner is nearest to overbalancing. By shifting your posture slightly further at this point you can become more firmly rooted, more immoveable.

NB The partners are labelled A and B; partner A is on the left in all the illustrations.

Starting

The partners begin facing one another, each standing with the right foot forward, so that the leading feet are side by side. The right hands are raised to chest height and the arms touch each other on the outer edges of the wrists. The left arms are raised, with the forearms at about waist height. (Throughout the exercise the "free" left arm acts as a counterbalance to movements on the right.)

1a *Partner B first turns his or her right hand over so that the palm faces the body, then gently pushes with the wrist against A's wrist, straight to the front of the body. To do this, B has to rock forward onto his or her right leg. A yields to this pressure and allows his or her wrist to be pushed back until the arm is folded close to the body, the hand at shoulder height. In yielding, A rocks the weight backward onto his or her left leg. Shifting weight in this way rotates the torso slightly.*

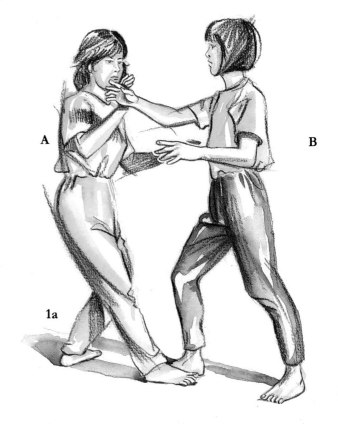

A   B

1a

1b *As B's weight is furthest forward and his or her arm is extended, A turns his or her own right hand over, so that the palm faces forward, and rests it on the back of B's right wrist.*

1b

1c *Now A begins to rock forward onto the right leg, pushing B's arm and weight back. A's torso rotates slightly to the left, bringing the right arm and shoulder forward, shifting the weight onto the right leg. B responds to this by yielding, just as A did in position 1a.*

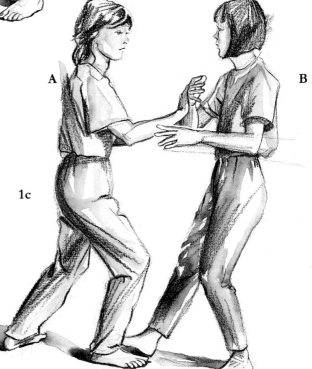

1c

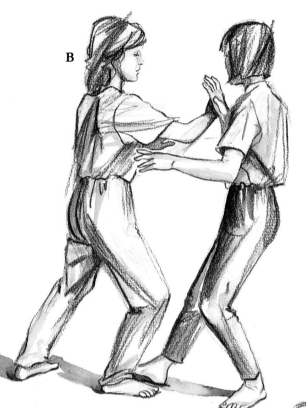

1d *As A reaches the forward position, B turns his or her own wrist over and begins to push A back again.*

1d

1e *A yields as B's energy moves forward again, and the partners repeat the sequence. Both parties sway to and fro, as if cutting logs together with a two-handled saw. This constant ebbing and flowing motion can be kept up for as long as the partners wish, but should be practised for at least 2-3 minutes. Some partners enjoy pushing hands for half an hour or more. When the right side tires, you can use the other side of the body so that the left arms and legs "lead".*

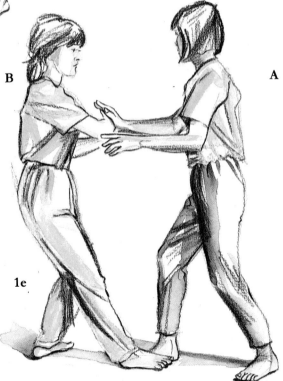

1e

PART TWO

The Balanced Way

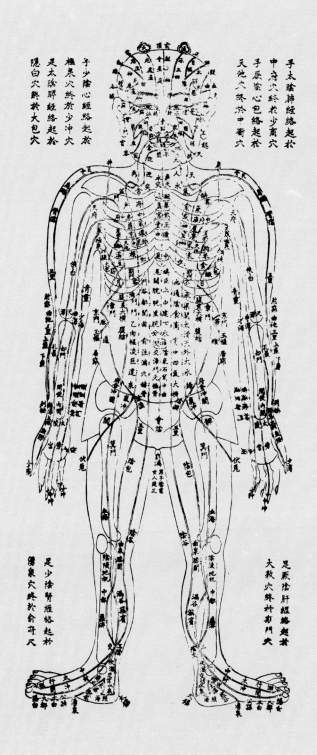

手太陰肺經絡起於
中府穴終於少商穴
手厥陰心包絡起於
天池穴終於中衝穴

手少陰心經絡起於
極泉穴終於少衝穴
足太陰脾經絡起於
隱白穴終於大包穴

足厥陰肝經絡起於
大敦穴終於期門穴

足少陰腎經絡起於
湧泉穴終於俞府穴

5: Oriental paths to balance

Once you have achieved a grounding in the practical side of the soft martial arts, you are ready for a deeper appraisal of the Way of Harmony. Practising the arts taught in Part One will in itself bring many benefits – but in China, where the arts originate, daily exercise is just one aspect of a whole lifestyle that should be harmonized in a number of different ways. This chapter shows how the Tao – the Way of the Universe – can form the basis of your whole lifestyle, helping you to become a more vibrant, calm, and balanced person.

Throughout China's history there has been a deep understanding of Man's place in the Universe, and a belief that Man should harmonize his life with the way of the natural world. This way is called Tao, and it is the source of everything (the history of Taoism is related on page 13 in the Introduction to this book). From this single concept flow all the philosophy and the practicalities of the soft martial arts. Tao gives you a sense of the interconnectedness of all things. This is soon apparent when you practise the soft arts. The T'ai Chi Short Form, for example, relates to many aspects of life – not only to the need for exercise, but to the health of body and mind, to self defence, to meditation and, not least, to spiritual awareness. But the Tao takes you even further than that. It teaches that every single area of life is fundamentally interconnected – not just exercise and mental and bodily health, but the condition of your vital organs, your predominant feelings and

emotions, sexual behaviour, the pattern of diet, the way you eat your food, your breathing, and your spiritual life.

Underlying all these different aspects of life are the concepts of Chi, or vital energy, and the Five Elements, the basic building blocks of the Universe. In order to achieve true balance, which is the primary aim of the soft martial artist, you need to learn how to modify your lifestyle in ways that will increase your Chi and balance the elements within you – which in turn will improve your performance in the soft arts.

In the West, few people enjoy the kind of lifestyle that can give a sense of wholeness – instead, most people live their lives in the face of forces that seem to pull them apart. Work rarely gives anybody the time to eat well or to take enough exercise; advertising constantly promotes images and desires that misrepresent what people really are; and healthcare services all too often proffer a pill for every ill rather than discovering the root causes of a patient's troubles.

The same is generally true of the way that the soft martial arts are taught in the West. The soft arts are often misrepresented, divorced from their true context, rather than being seen as an integral part of a well-balanced lifestyle. This chapter reveals something of the context from which the soft arts were born and teaches you how to integrate the Taoist wisdom that underlies the arts into your daily life – leading you to that feeling of wholeness and balance which is the real Way of Harmony.

A deeper look at Chi

In learning the soft arts you will already have seen how the fundamental concepts of Chi and the Five Elements underlie the theory and practice of Chi Kung, Hsing I, Pa Kua, and T'ai Chi Chuan, and how they are used as guides to help you improve your performance and face an opponent more effectively. But these concepts are also firmly rooted in all important aspects of Chinese culture – they form the basis of traditional cosmology, as well as of Chinese medicine, and the Chinese approach to diet.

Understanding more about them will not only increase your appreciation of the soft arts, it will also provide an invaluable frame of reference through which you can interpret the world around you.

Chi is the root of all energy. It is what drives the wind and gives the sun its power. It is what makes plants, animals, and people grow, reproduce, and flourish. It is breath itself, the air you breathe and the vital energy you get from breathing it. And it is in order to maximize Chi that you pay special attention to ways in which you can control your breathing while training in the soft arts (pp.167-9). Exactly the same care is paid to controlling energy flow in Yoga, meditation, and all the other "deep" training systems.

In the soft arts, many exercises are designed to teach you to store Chi in your own body, at the Tan Tien, the body's energy centre in the lower abdomen (p.24). Other more advanced techniques teach students to concentrate the vital energy in particular spots in the body, to produce extraordinary strength and resistance from attack at these points. It is said that the most advanced masters can transmit Chi to other people, using it defensively or therapeutically, and indeed, Chi Kung is used to this end in many hospitals in China today.

To begin to understand how this is possible, it helps to look more deeply at how the Chinese believe the human body works. One of the earliest discoveries that China's medical sages recorded is that, like the Universe as a whole, the parts of the human body are divided into two fundamental groups, the Yin and the Yang, and are associated with the Five Elements (pp.151-3). The many aspects of personality are also interpreted in this light, as shown right and on page 162.

Yin and Yang
What are the characteristics of these two basic qualities? They originally referred to the dark (Yin) side of a mountain and to the sunlit (Yang) side. To the Chinese, Yin qualities are more female, dark, solid, substantial, negative, cool, and tending to move downward. Things that are Yang are the reverse – more masculine, light, immaterial, positive, warm, and tending to move upward. People's characters can also be interpreted according to Yin and Yang. There are those who are very Yang – thin busy types who are always rushing around, who can't sleep well, and who sometimes seem to lack a centre to their lives. Then there are those in whom Yin predominates – the relaxed, sleepy types who sometimes seem lethargic and even indifferent.

Understanding the elements

The Five Elements are the fundamental components of
the Universe – Water, Wood, Fire, Earth, and Metal.
Many of the forms of the soft arts are shaped around the
flow of Chi through the elements. And in Hsing I (p.46),
the elements themselves are transformed into human
motion – into a series of interconnected actions which
dramatically relate to one another.

The Chinese also relate these cosmic elements to the
human body – to the meridians and vital organs (p.152),
as well as to your emotional responses (p.162). In
addition to these bodily aspects, each element is
associated with, among other things, a colour, a sound, a
smell, a taste, a season, and a time of day. By using these
indicators with care, you can learn to understand your
own elemental composition. Colour, for example, helps
to identify elemental attractions and repulsions –
everyone tends to like certain colours and dislike others.
Similarly, you may feel good or bad at certain times of
the day. (The time of day linked to each element relates
to when the associated organs are most active.)

In healthy people, the elements are balanced; in sick
people they are unbalanced. Indications of an imbalance
may appear in signs as varied as an unusual skin colour
or body odour, or in the recurrence of a particular
symptom at specific times of day or year. Checking signs
like these helps the Chinese physician to determine
which element is unbalanced and thus to understand
how to treat the problem.

The Five Elements
Each element has its special
associations, ranging from
particular organs in the
human body, to colours,
flavours, and so forth, as
shown below.

	Water	Wood	Fire	Earth	Metal
Meridians and organs	Kidneys Bladder	Liver Gall Bladder	Heart Heart protector Small intestine Triple beater	Spleen Stomach	Lungs Large intestine
Colour	Blue/black	Green	Red	Yellow	White
Sound	Groaning	Shouting	Laughing	Singing	Weeping
Smell	Putrid	Rancid	Scorched	Fragrant	Rotten
Taste	Salty	Sour	Bitter	Sweet	Pungent
Emotion	Fear	Anger	Joy	Sympathy	Grief
Season	Winter	Spring	Summer	Late summer	Autumn
Time of day	3-7 pm	11pm-1 am	11am-3 pm, 7-11 pm	7-11 am	3-7 am

Vital organs and meridians

The human body contains five pairs of vital organs, each of which is correlated with one of the elements. The elements as organs nourish us and perform all the functions of sustaining life. Thus one Earth organ, the stomach, "ripens and rots" your food, while its sister organ, the spleen, helps with this and transports the food on to the next stage in the digestive cycle.

As Chi flows through the body, it follows a number of special channels called meridians. Among the most important are those which pass through the five pairs of vital organs. These either carry energy to the organs or carry the energy which the organs produce to other areas of the body. Thus the meridians stretch all over the body, linking apparently unrelated areas such as ears, arms, or feet to the vital organs in the centre of the body, such as the kidneys, heart, or stomach. In addition to the five pairs of vital organ meridians, there are four other major meridians – the Heart Protector and Triple Heater (both Fire meridians) and the Governing and Conception Vessels (p.165).

Over the centuries, Chinese physicians discovered that at certain points along the meridians the insertion of a needle or the application of pressure could be used to balance and regulate the flow of Chi – thus preventing or curing a wide variety of ailments and disabilities. This is the basis of acupuncture and acupressure, and, in Japan, of the therapy Shiatsu.

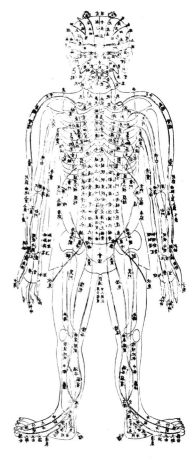

Meridians and vital organs
The paths of the five pairs of meridians pass through the organs they are named after. These are some of the body's chief Chi pathways. Together the five pairs of organs – one Yin, one Yang in each pair – perform all the functions of sustaining the life force, regulating your breathing, heartbeat, digestion, and metabolism.

Cycles of energy

The Five Elements relate to one another via the cycles of creation and control. In the Cycle of Creation, Chi flows unceasingly from one element to the next. Water transforms into Wood to make it grow. Wood burns, creating Fire, which in turn makes ash, which feeds the Earth. Earth condenses under pressure to form Metal, which generates Water.

In the Cycle of Control, arranged as a five-pointed star, each element balances or exerts a controlling influence over its successor. Thus Water, at the start of the cycle, controls Fire: too much moisture damps it down, too little, and fire will blaze up out of control. Physically, this may show as water retention, overloading the heart, or kidney failure leading to high blood pressure. Wood controls Earth: normally the Wood organs (liver, gall bladder) aid the Earth organs (spleen, stomach) in digesting food. But too much control – Wood over-controlling or attacking Earth – may result in indigestion or ulcers. Fire controls Metal, producing appropriate warmth, and Earth in its turn restrains Water (the image is of earth banks controlling water channels, as the spleen controls body fluids). Finally, Metal checks Wood, just as "ten deep breaths" activates the lungs and controls anger rising from the liver.

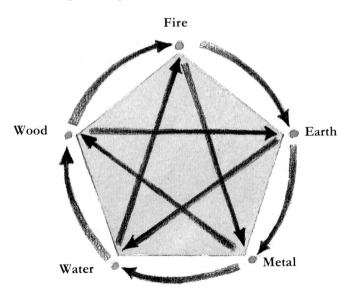

A balanced diet

It is a truism that you are what you eat. Yet there is no doubt that food does more than simply recharge the body. Health, mood, alertness, and many other aspects of life are affected by what you eat, how you eat it, and how your food has been prepared. Most Westerners have a poor understanding of the relationship between the quality of food and the quality of life, but the Chinese have studied these processes for millennia. The oldest medical text in China says: "The superior physician treats disease before it arises, using only the right food." The traditional Chinese understanding of the properties of food is sometimes referred to as macrobiotics, but in fact macrobiotics is a modern Japanese formulation which bears little resemblance to Chinese knowledge, and in some cases conflicts with it.

This section gives a broad outline of the basic Chinese approach to food, with guidelines on how to achieve balance and improve health through a careful choice of ingredients (taking into account their special properties, see facing page), and through good methods of preparation, combined with a balanced manner of serving and eating at mealtimes (p.161).

Everybody should try to balance his or her diet according to the principles of Yin (cool or cold) and Yang (ranging from warm to hot). The "four natures" or temperatures of many different foods are shown on pages 156-161. Adjusting your diet to the seasons is also important, and ensuring that the staple foods in your diet are nutritous (see Earth nourishment, right).

You should consider your special needs and the needs of those for whom you are cooking. As you change through life, so too your diet should change. A baby's delicate digestion cannot tolerate excessively hot or cold foods. "Roughage foods", essential for adults, are not at all suited to small children. In adolescence, while lots of food is needed to help with the process of rapid growth, too much greasy or oily food may well produce heat and toxins, leading to skin problems. In adult life, diet should be wide ranging and well-balanced, giving you strength and resilience, while as the body ages and tends to "cool down", the diet may need adjusting to a weaker digestive ability – and may come once again closer to the needs of childhood.

Earth nourishment
As a general rule it is good to centre the diet around those foods that will form a core of nourishment and strengthen your stomach, helping you to gain the most from what you eat. Foods that relate to the Earth element are very helpful. Earth is associated with a sweet taste (p.151). Rice relates to Earth – as do many other everyday foods such as beef, potatoes, chicken, carrots, cabbage, corn, apples, and bananas, although each of these foods has a unique set of characteristics – actions, temperature, and so forth.

Properties and categories of food

Chinese experts analyse the nature of foods in many different ways. The Yin and Yang aspect of foods, which is most important in terms of the balance of a healthy diet, is mainly implied by their temperature or nature. The predominant element of foods is revealed by their flavour – for example, most salty foods are Yin and they are associated with Water and the kidneys (see below). Foods also have an affinity for those meridians that are related to the element and its vital organs. On this basis Chinese experts have developed prescriptions for the best types of foods to eat for any particular condition. This understanding can easily be applied to ingredients in the Western diet too. Categories of foods, such as vegetables and dairy products, are analysed on pages 156-61 according to these properties.

Four natures
The first property which all foods have is temperature (hot, warm, neutral, cool, and cold). This covers the spectrum from Yang (hot and warm) to Yin (cool and cold). Hot foods heat you up, cold foods cool you down. Neutral foods will neither heat you up nor cool you down, and therefore can be used without causing imbalance in the diet. It is best to avoid extremes and keep an overall balance.

Flavours
The flavours (salty, sour, bitter, sweet, and pungent/spicy) follow the Five Element cycle (p.151), and indicate which of the vital organs is most affected by a food. Saltiness (Yin, Water) tends to soften and lubricate; it is linked to the kidneys. Sourness (Yin, Wood), associated with the liver, is more tightening and absorbent. Bitter flavours (Yin, Fire), related to the heart, are drying and purging. Sweetness (Yang, Earth) goes mostly to the spleen and stomach where it is used to build up the body. Finally, pungent foods (Yang, Metal) affect the lungs, dispersing – often through sweating – and helping energy and blood to flow.

Four directions
The four directions (ascending, descending, floating, and sinking) indicate how a food makes the Chi flow through your body. Hot and warm foods and Yang-flavoured foods tend to move the energy up and out. Cold, cool, and Yin-flavoured foods have the opposite effect. Foods that are light tend to make energy float or rise, while heavy foods such as roots and fruits make your energy sink or descend.

Medicinal properties
Foods are known to have a therapeutic function, and herbs in particular have very specific uses. Garlic, ginger, and rosemary, for example, are said to tone and regulate the Chi, expel cold, and sedate Yin. Garlic is used for many digestive ailments. Ginger is often helpful if a cold is starting. Rosemary can be used for premature baldness and certain types of headaches.

Grains and legumes

Neutral – aduki beans, corn, kidney beans, rice, rye
Cool – barley, buckwheat, millet, soybean, wheat

Grains have always been at the heart of the Chinese diet. In China, rice is a symbol for nourishment itself. Grains fall mainly into the cool and neutral categories and most have a strengthening and balancing effect on the system. Ideally, they should play a large part in the diet. Each grain also has special characteristics of its own.

Corn may be prescribed to help heart disease and sexual weakness, rice is helpful in diarrhoea, and rye, which is more bitter in flavour (and thus most helpful to the Fire organs – the heart and the small intestine), is often prescribed to aid migraine sufferers. Wheat, barley, buckwheat and millet are more Yin in quality, since they are cool, and they have a descending action which favours the kidneys and intestines. They can be used on their own for "hot" people – those who have predominantly Yang rather than Yin characteristics (see Yin and Yang, p.150) – and in hot weather. But for children and those with more delicate or cooler constitutions, they should be balanced with warmer foods – especially in winter.

Of the legumes, aduki and kidney beans both help to strengthen the Yin in the body while also helping to clear excess fluids and swellings. Soybeans also strengthen Yin, but at the same time they are good for clearing out chills. Their consumption is useful in a wide range of conditions, including diarrhoea, skin eruptions, and emaciation, but eating too many may overload the digestive system and lead to stagnant Chi, with excess mucus, a yellowish complexion, and feelings of bloatedness and heaviness. A small but regular amount of beans in the diet helps to keep the system clean.

Fish

Hot – trout
Warm – anchovies, mussels, shrimps
Neutral – herring, mackerel, oysters, sardines, tuna, white fish
Cold – crab, octopus

Fish have a wide range of temperatures and actions and they are more often forbidden in the diet by Chinese physicians than most other foods.

Crab, a cold food, is very helpful in clearing heat from the body (though it will not control a temperature related to an infection). Trout, on the other hand, is hot and can be helpful if a person is cold. But too much may produce hot and itchy skin eruptions – and the same goes for octopus, herring, and some other sea foods, which in the West are recognized as provoking allergic reactions. Mussels and anchovies are warm and tonify the Chi. Mussels in particular have an effect on the kidneys, therefore also influencing all conditions where there is weakness in the lower back and lower abdomen. They tend to be prescribed for a great range of ailments, from vertigo and night sweating to lumbago and abdominal pain. Herring, mackerel, and white fish are more neutral, having a wide tonifying effect. White fish affect the lungs, stomach, and liver, and are used to relieve indigestion and improve a poor appetite. Herring and mackerel are often used to help people who are suffering from exhaustion. Mackerel has the further benefit of aiding the kind of rheumatism that gets worse when the weather is damp. Oysters are used in Chinese medicine to tonify the Yin, and to remedy insomnia, nervousness, and indecisiveness. Like sardines and shrimps, they also have a strengthening effect on the digestion, and warm the stomach. But they should not be taken if you have a temperature, or if you are a predominantly Yang, or hot, person.

Meat and eggs

Hot – mutton
Neutral – beef, duck, lamb, pork, beef liver, eggs
Warm – chicken, lamb kidney, chicken liver

In general, meats have a strengthening effect on the Chi and the blood – hence the beef tea and chicken broth for convalescents. Most are from neutral to warm, and most have a sweet flavour (Earth), thus tending to warm and strengthen the stomach and spleen – though they should not be eaten in large quantities. Mutton, as its nature is hot, is indicated where a person has symptoms of cold, such as cold abdominal pain, or is feeling chilled after having a baby. It is not suitable for anybody suffering from hot symptoms. Pork is neutral, sweet, and salty – it is said to lubricate dryness, and is used to treat dry coughs and constipation. Of the organ meats, kidneys benefit the kidneys, and liver benefits the liver. Any debilitating condition or poor overall health is improved by good broths made of duck, beef, or chicken.

Chicken eggs are neutral and sweet, strengthening the Chi and the blood. They are often used to treat dry coughs, sore throats, and conjunctivitis.

Dairy products

Warm – butter
Neutral – cow's milk, human milk

In general, the Chinese do not use dairy products in their diet – in fact cheese is practically unheard of in most areas of China. This is partly because they are not available in many areas, but also because they are known to provoke excess mucus. The Chinese say that they are "damp" producing. All types of dairy products should be avoided when a person is suffering from a cough or phlegmy cold. However, cow's milk can be used to treat some conditions; it is neutral in nature and sweet in flavour, and acts as a tonic for the stomach and lungs, since it produces fluids and thus lubricates the intestines. Human milk is used as a blood tonic and as a lubricant for internal dryness. Butter is warm and sweet, and affects many internal organs.

Dairy products tend to be high in cholesterol and eating too much contributes to overweight, heart problems, and many related conditions. Most people in the West eat far too much of these foods.

Fruits and nuts

Warm – cherry, chestnut, peach, pine nuts, strawberry, walnut
Neutral – almond, coconut, figs, grapes, olives, peanuts, pineapple, plum, raspberry
Cool – apple, pear, tangerine
Cold – banana, watermelon

Most fruits and nuts are sweet, though some – like olives, peaches, and plums – are also sour. This means that they tend to have most effect on the digestive system. The sweet flavour affects the stomach and the spleen; the sour affects the liver. Many fruit, such as bananas, peaches, and pears, create moisture in the system, lubricating the intestines. Peanuts have a similar effect. Some fruits are particularly helpful for hot, dry lungs – among them almonds, olives, peaches, pears, tangerines, and watermelon. It is very important to be aware of these effects when you are eating fruit or nuts, for too much will create too much moisture, which can lead to diarrhoea or excess mucus in the lungs (peanuts eaten in large quantities are particularly damaging).

Fruits can be very useful in cooling down – and the coldest ones have the most dramatic effect. Just try drinking a glassful of watermelon juice after a fiery curry or chilli dish!

Along with apple and pineapple, these cool and cold fruits are most useful in treating the effects of heat stroke. They will therefore often have a bad effect – such as diarrhoea or a severe stomach ache – if eaten in large quantities, especially if the person is a bit cold to start with. These properties are most obvious in relation to more delicate digestive systems, such as those of young children – bananas, for example, may provoke painful colic.

Several fruits are noted for their tonic effects. Taking grapes to someone who is recovering from an illness is a recognition of this power. But you should always be careful when choosing fruits for convalescents – cold fruits, or those that are difficult to digest, such as plums and cherries, would be inadvisable. In general, the rule about being careful not to eat too much of any food of either extreme of temperature applies very much to fruits.

Most nuts are less extreme in their actions, and several types of nut are considered highly nutritious. Coconuts, for example, which are neutral, are used to help children suffering from malnutrition. And chestnuts, which are warm and sweet, nourish the kidneys, and are sometimes used to treat nausea. Pine nuts, also warm and sweet, benefit the lungs, large intestine, and liver. Walnuts, which sedate Yin and tonify the kidneys, are commonly used to treat asthma, coughs, lumbago, and impotence.

Seasonal fruits (right)
The natural cycles of local produce still predominate in less developed regions in China. Whatever is in season is most likely to be right for a balanced diet at the time of year.

Vegetables

Warm – leek, onion
Neutral – beet, cabbage, carrot, peas, potatoes, pumpkin, turnip, yam
Cool – celery, cucumber, lettuce, mushroom, radish, spinach, watercress
Cold – asparagus, bamboo shoots, tomato

Generally, vegetables have fewer contra-indications than other foods (in the West we would say they cause fewer strong allergic reactions) and they have a wide range of uses. Summer vegetables are cooling, so they are suitable for warm or hot weather, while root vegetables are warming, and therefore best for the winter months. Vegetable soups, as long as they are chosen with due care, can have a wonderfully beneficial effect in all kinds of conditions.

Many vegetables have specific effects on the digestion, ranging from the warming effects of cabbage, leeks, turnips, and yams, which all help if someone is cold (and perhaps has diarrhoea), to the coolness of celery, cucumber, mushrooms, radish, tomato, and watercress. Be careful of giving children too much cucumber and tomato – these cooling vegetables may very easily chill their vulnerable digestions and provoke colic or diarrhoea. Celery is also cool and goes further on this path – it is indicated in the early stages of hypertension and for irrational rages. The cool vegetables have very many clinical uses – for instance, cucumber alleviates thirst, relieves mental depression, and is used to treat sore throats, conjunctivitis, and burns. Some vegetables are cold – like asparagus, which is valuable in the treatment of any illness where excess heat is present, such as diabetes, and hot, dry constipation. The cold vegetables are contra-indicated when a person feels very cold. Warm vegetables come into their own in the winter season. In the early stages of a cold, the humble onion is very useful, helping you to sweat out the infection. Cabbage is warming, and promotes digestion. Other vegetables have specific effects on particular parts of the body – spinach can help with any tendency to bleeding and also nourishes the blood; beet and radish clear the diaphragm and chest, and the common potato is highly regarded by the Chinese as an excellent tonic for the kidneys – and of benefit to the virile organs.

Herbs, spices, condiments, sugar

Hot – black pepper, cayenne pepper
Warm – basil, brown sugar, cardamom, coriander, fennel seed, garlic, mustard, nutmeg, rosemary, vinegar
Neutral – white sugar
Cool – marjoram, peppermint
Cold – salt

Herbs, spices, and condiments are an essential part of cooking, and their use can come close to Chinese herbal medicine itself. Properly used, herbs and spices can balance dishes and adjust them to suit the individual, the time of day, or the time of year. Many herbs are also well-known medicines and the actions ascribed to them are often complex. Herbalists may prescribe them in large doses, but in food they should be used in small amounts – enough to harmonize the dishes and to enhance digestion. There are times when a herb or spice is contra-indicated by the herbalist. If you are too hot, for example, the hot and warm spices will not be suitable. Spices are nearly all pungent in flavour, which means that they will have a particular effect on the lungs, clearing congestion and cleansing the whole system. They are useful in general, but especially so in the early stages of a feverish illness such as flu.

Preparing and eating food

Apart from the theory of food properties, there are many more practical and important aspects to a balanced diet, and the Chinese have a distinctive approach not only in preparation and cooking, but in serving and eating food. As with all things based on the Way, you should avoid going to extremes which might upset your balance in the opposite direction. For example, beware of eating too much of any one food, or of a food that is very hot or very cold. Variety in your diet is a key to balance. The Chinese provide a selection of different dishes at each meal, which ensures that everyone at the table takes in a broad spectrum of different vitamins, minerals, and other elements that are essential for good health. Expert Chinese cooks will actually "balance" the contents of each dish in terms of the properties of the ingredients, the cooking method, and the accompanying sauces, herbs, or spices. But in broader terms it is possible to plan your meals in a balanced way, so that hot foods are accompanied by cool ones, sour is balanced with sweet, and so on. The quality of food – the freshness of vegetables, fruit, fish and meat – is also of the essence.

Generally, the Chinese spend more time preparing food and less time cooking it than people do in the West. Cutting food into small pieces makes it easier to handle, chew, and digest. And food can be cooked very quickly if it is cut up in small pieces, thus allowing less deterioration and loss of nutrients in cooking. Never gorge yourself – this is usually best achieved by stopping eating before you feel full. Excess food only overloads the digestive system. Meals take longer in China than in the West, but the food eaten is properly absorbed and the digestive organs are not abused. Most Chinese are careful to take their meals at regular times, and communal mealtimes with all members of the family together are an important part of life. Everyone ensures that the young and old people receive the best food for them. And each person also feels responsible for what he or she eats. Making food for each other, eating it together and sharing food are some of the oldest patterns of human culture, and they nourish more than just the body. Always bear in mind that food is not only good to eat, it is good to think about, and to share.

Chinese cooking methods
In China, steaming is a popular way to cook vegetables or fish, since it retains more nutrients. Meat is rarely roasted, since this adds unnecessary Yang heat and unhealthy fat. Frying is always done very quickly, with smoking hot oil, so the food rarely soaks up unhealthy amounts of fat and it tends to retain its texture.

Balancing your emotions

A heightened sense of calm and control is one of the first results of training in the soft arts. At all times you get a sense of being more in control of yourself and your destiny, and you become more sensitive to the feelings of those around you.

Most people have an affinity with one of the Five Elements (p.151) and its associated emotions. The Chinese identify two sorts of emotion for each element, one positive, the other negative (as shown, right), and these emotions relate to each other according to the cycles of the elements (p.153).

Water endows you with will, the drive to become. It is also the force of ambition and governs how well you "flow" through life, avoiding obstacles and overcoming challenges. You will feel fear most strongly when Water is in trouble. In the Cycle of Creation, Water's will and ambition lead naturally to the ability to plan and to control your future.

Wood is deeply concerned with creation, structure, and form, and the creation of boundaries and shape in life. You need only look at a child who is given no sense of routine and no boundaries to see why the negative side of Wood is said to be anger.

Fire endows you with the capacity for joy. It is the happiness and *joie de vivre* that you can feel radiating from others, or the warmth you feel when you are with someone you love. Once extinguished, its loss is visible in the person who has lost all joy, and a major loss can even stop the heart.

Earth gives a sense of security and groundedness, feeling solid, and having a place to be. It gives permanence to Fire's joy – without Earth, Fire has no place to burn. Earth also enables you to feel for other people and understand how you can be of use to others. If someone is always saying: "You poor thing", then it is their Earth that is in trouble.

From Earth comes Metal, the element that lets you realize the quality in yourself, in others, and in the world. It gives you the value of everything – without it, your sense of loss would be overpowering. But Metal can also lead to an endless search for meaning in life, for gurus who inevitably fail to match expectations.

Water (Kidneys)
Will, ambition, firmness
Terror, fear

Wood (Liver)
Creative urge
Anger, resentment, or frustration

Fire (Heart)
Joy
Lack of joy and love

Earth (Stomach)
Concern and empathy, concentration, memory
Worry, inappropriate or excessive sympathy

Metal (Lungs)
Grief, sense of value
Excessive or inappropriate grief; sense of lack or loss

The cycles of emotions
In the creation cycle each element feeds its neighbour with positive or negative emotions. Fear produces anger, but will and ambition can generate growth in Wood. In the control cycle, one state balances another, either constructively or destructively – joy can temper sadness, but lack of joy will allow grief to predominate.

Relating in harmony (right)
Neighbouring elements such as Fire and Earth, may make particularly harmonious partners.

Sexual balance

When practised in a balanced way, sex is a highly beneficial part of life, bringing us into greater harmony with each other and with the outside world. But all too often lack of understanding and knowledge lead to sexual problems and imbalance in men and women alike. Taoist masters have a highly developed understanding of sexual processes, and the philosophy of the soft arts incorporates special teachings about sexuality.

Developing the sexual arts can take place alongside the soft arts' training – indeed the Chinese themselves refer to this as sexual Kung Fu. "Jing", or vital sexual energy, is another form of Chi, and ultimately both arts are about developing the Chi energy system. (The Chinese also have many prescriptions for maintaining normal, healthy sex lives – these include exercises and herbal and other remedies to increase potency.

In the Chinese view, the piercing of an egg by a sperm cell is the original act of sexual Kung Fu in the battle of Yin and Yang. According to traditional theory, Jing is the source of all human life – it produces sperm and ova and is stored in the kidneys. Any practice that regulates the flow of this energy is beneficial to health and well-being. Jing is seen as a pure, almost volatile form of energy that is easily transformed into other types of Chi and then circulated to other parts of the body.

There are two schools of thought in Taoism about how to regulate Jing. One maintains that a balanced sex life ("regulating the affairs of the bedroom") helps you to achieve longevity and health. The alternative school advocates extreme restraint. The retention of sperm, whether achieved through abstinence or by averting ejaculation, is seen as the key to spiritual development and to longevity. Once again the masters are concerned with Chi, but in this case the aim is to convert the Jing into other types of Chi, to nourish the body and the spirit. As with other spiritual training systems, when you learn the soft martial arts you may come to feel that you want to abstain from sex for a while. Abstinence can certainly concentrate and develop your Chi – and many people who aim to enrich their relationship with their partner through a well-balanced sex life have found that a period of abstinence has its benefits.

The inner energy orbit

When your Jing or sexual energy is converted into Chi it flows along two primary meridians – the Conception Vessel and Governing Vessel. These are of fundamental importance to your energy flow since they connect all your vital organs and glands and your spinal column. Together the two channels carry the sexual current – Jing converted to Chi – from the genitals, spreading vitality throughout the body. In fact, energy can flow up or down the individual vessels. It can also flow around the channels in a loop or orbit, in both directions. This refreshes your body and gives you more energy to develop your spiritual power.

The deep pathway (above)
The deep pathway runs in an S-shaped curve from the tongue to the perineum. This creates a Yin-Yang division – the front is Yin, the back is Yang.

Energizing the inner orbit
One way to open the orbit is simply to sit in meditation for a few minutes, letting your mind travel around the orbit (far right), sensing the flow of Chi.

There is also an excellent breathing exercise, which opens the orbit, as described below. It will help, however, if you practise some breathing techniques (pp.167-9) before you attempt this. The aim is to sensitize yourself to the flow of Chi, and great concentration is needed to guide the Chi along the correct pathway, to enable the feeling of the energy flow to develop. You inhale as you follow the Governing (Yang) Vessel and exhale as you follow the Conception (Yin) Vessel. Start with a slow inhalation. The Chi enters your body as air through your nose. Feel it rise up between your eyes, over your forehead and scalp until it reaches the top of your skull.

Feel the tingling and lightness there. Then follow the energy as it goes down the back of your skull and into your spine, down to the base and then on to the perineum, between your legs. It swirls forward to the Tan Tien at the end of breathing in. (Although the meridians meet at the perineum, this exercise requires that you start exhaling at the Tan Tien.) As you begin to exhale, feel the Chi uncurl from the Tan Tien and begin to rise slowly within you – up through the stomach, past the solar plexus, into the lungs and out through the mouth, emerging as warm, moist breath.

Keep the tip of your tongue touching the roof of your mouth to complete the circuit and allow the Chi to flow all around the body. (This is why you practise the T'ai Chi Short Form – and other soft arts exercises – with your tongue touching the roof of your mouth.)

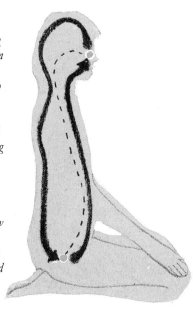

Surface pathways (below)
The Governing Vessel runs along the spine and over the skull; the Conception Vessel bisects the front of the body.

Meditation and breathing

To practise any of the martial arts taught in Part One is in a sense to undertake a form of spiritual training, for the soft arts lead you naturally to the centre of your being: your spirit or soul. You are learning to balance and harmonize your whole being, your body, mind, and soul. Perhaps the most direct way you come into contact with the spirit is through the understanding of Chi flow through the body, which you develop as you practise the "moving meditation" of the soft arts' exercises. You can also experience the flow of Chi while you are practising static meditation, and in this way increase your sensitivity to it. Chi nourishes the spirit – harmonizing your energy flow and helping you to order and develop your mind. The mind is the gateway to the spirit.

Practised daily, even for a short time, meditation builds a pool of calm strength inside you. The mind is rested, the body relaxed, and the flow of breath and blood improves. You can meditate in many different circumstances, for instance while you are travelling on buses or trains, or at intervals in your work. It can be practised perfectly well sitting upright in a chair, with your feet flat on the floor – or sitting cross-legged on the ground, or kneeling as if in prayer. If you are a naturally tense person, it may help if you do a little Chi Kung or T'ai Chi exercise before you start.

Starting to meditate
It's best to choose the same time each day for your practice. Choose a place where you won't be disturbed, and sit or kneel in your chosen posture. Breathe slowly, deeply, and naturally, using your diaphragm. (This is basic Yang breathing, p.25.) Try to empty your mind of worries and pressing concerns, and be calm and composed within yourself. Finding this frame of mind will get easier with practice, but it may help if you use a focal object or sound to help you concentrate – Indians and Tibetans use the sacred word OM repeated over and over again. A mandala, a complex visual symbol, is also used as a focal point.

Keep breathing slowly and deeply until you feel completely calm. Once you are in a true meditative state, try to remain with it for some time. You shouldn't need to decide on a length of time for your practice since the whole aim is to teach you to go beyond the narrow linear measures of time and space to a plane where a minute is much the same as an hour or a moment. When you have felt this, even fleetingly, you have made great progress.

Kneeling position
The most common meditation position adopted by martial arts' performers is a simple kneeling pose. You can sit on your heels, as shown right, or between them, with your bottom on the floor, and your hands on your thighs.

Breathing exercises

Breathing should be the only conscious activity which takes place during meditation, and its control is central to developing your ability to concentrate. The Taoists identify many advanced breathing techniques – such as the exercise shown on page 165, and Six Sounds breathing, page 169 – that are used to maintain health and to cure diseases of the inner organs, among other benefits. But there are three simple, fundamental types: Yin; Yang; and Yin-Yang.

The first is Yin breathing – this is shallow breathing characterized by an inflated ribcage and by the shoulders rising and sinking with each breath. This is how many adults breathe – but it is a poor way of taking oxygen into the body, and does little else for you. There is a variant of Yin breathing though which, when practised correctly, can have important benefits (see below). Yang breathing – deep regular inhalation and exhalation using the diaphragm – is taught on page 25. It requires you to push your diaphragm downward as you inhale so that it massages the internal organs. This is used in meditation and is helpful in balancing the flow of Chi (a further Yang exercise is shown on the following page).

Yin breathing exercise
This exercise is very relaxing. Sit down and rest your right elbow on a table. Put your right index finger on your forehead, between your eyes. Then close your right nostril with your right thumb and inhale until your chest is full, then exhale just as slowly until all the air has gone. Now release your right nostril and close your left one, using your right middle finger. Breathe in and out again slowly. Repeat this 5 times.

Yang breathing exercise

A *Stand with your feet about shoulder's width apart. As you breathe in strongly through your nose, raise your hands, palms forward, in front of your shoulders. Exhale slowly but forcefully through your mouth and, as you do so, push your hands straight forward, palms forward, until your arms are fully extended in front of you.*

B *Breathe in again through the nose and allow your hands to return in front of your shoulders. This time, as you exhale through your mouth, push your hands out to either side.*

C *Breathe in through your nose and return your hands to your shoulders. Then exhale through your mouth, and push both your hands upward.*

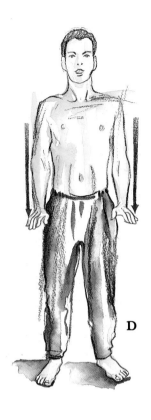

D *Finally, breathe in again, returning your hands to your shoulders, and exhale as you push them downward. Repeat the whole series of breaths and arm movements once again.*

D

Yin-Yang breathing

Either sitting in a chair or on the floor, place your right hand on your Tan Tien and your left hand on your solar plexus (just above your stomach). Keep both hands in direct contact with your body. Breathe in deeply through the nose, feeling the air pushing your right hand out. Hold your breath, then push in with your right hand, pushing the air up to the solar plexus. Now press with your left hand, forcing the air up into your chest. Continue exhaling slowly until your chest is deflated, empty of air. When you have finished exhaling, press in again gently, first with your left hand, then with your right. Only then should you take a new breath. Repeat the exercise at least 5 times.

Six Sounds breathing

Each sound benefits a particular vital organ, and is used to cure ailments related to the organ as well as to protect it from disease. To keep all the related organs healthy, you should practise each sound 5-10 times every day. First sit yourself down on a chair or on the ground with your back upright. Then pronounce the sounds with strong aspiration while exhaling quickly, but not too forcefully. If one of the organs is diseased, its sound should be repeated 36 times in succession.

Six Sounds

Kidneys	FU
Liver	SHU
Heart	HA
Spleen	HU
Lungs	SSSS
Solar plexus	SHI*

* *pronounced SHE*

Finding your balance

As you progress in the soft arts you will find that your awareness of your own being changes. You gain a better sense of your body, of its size, shape, and weight. Your balance improves, and you find yourself carrying out everyday tasks with the appropriate amount of energy, not too much or too little. Your movements become more economical, and you can find that you perform even awkward tasks without risk of strain or injury. Your mind grows too, becoming calmer, more detached – but also more sensitive to your own and to other people's states of mind.

Your increasing knowledge of the soft arts will protect you well in any situation where fighting takes place. But there are many other advantages to having a trained body and mind. For example, if you use a T'ai Chi step back, like step 3b from the 24-step Short Form (p.96), when you need to lift something heavy from the ground, the position of your feet and your weight distribution will help you move without risk of strain. Similarly, if you are standing in a crowded bus or train, struggling to retain your balance, you can adopt the rooted foot and leg posture of T'ai Chi step 9b (p.110). And when you need to push a piece of furniture or even a car, or lift something heavy from waist height, you can rely on the pushing movements which occur throughout the Short Form. If you experiment with the postures and moves you have learned from Part One, you will appreciate how they can be integrated into your daily life. It is when they have become part of the way that you do things, naturally, without a second thought, that you begin to really appreciate the Way of Harmony.

When you are walking, try to feel light and springy, not dull and heavy – think of the Chi Kung exercise walking on page 42. Walking is a fine form of exercise, and you should do as much of it as you can, especially if your work keeps you deskbound. Swimming and jogging are also useful and complementary forms of exercise. Even when you are just standing, try to feel the lightness of your being, not its weight. If you have to spend time standing on one spot, put your weight first on one foot, then on the other – this will help your circulation. Similarly, if you sit down, don't slouch, and don't stay still for too long. Every hour or so get up, stretch, and do a little exercise. And, when you sleep, don't lie stretched out prone, but curl yourself slightly. This will help to keep your joints relaxed and unstrained.

There are many more advantages to be gained if you succeed in integrating the teachings of this chapter into your daily life. You can use your own reactions to Yin and Yang and the Five Elements to modify your diet and eating habits, and to try to achieve better balance in your relationships. There is no need to hide away the deeper side of yourself, which this book is trying to develop. You should note, though, that the exercises and prescriptions in this chapter may show you the way to achieve harmony – but it is you who must walk down that path; you who must teach yourself, through practice, the sense of unity, calmness, and spiritual awareness which the Way of Harmony offers.

He who is endowed with ample virtue may be compared to
  an infant.
No venomous insects sting him;
Nor fierce beasts seize him;
Nor birds of prey strike him;
His bones are frail, his sinews tender, but his grasp is strong.
He does not know the conjugation of male and female, and yet
  he has sexual development;
It means he is in the best vitality.
He may cry all day long without growing hoarse;
It means that he is in the perfect harmony.
To know this harmony is to approach eternity;
To know eternity is to attain enlightenment.

From Lao Tzu's *Tao Te Ching*

摩腎堂圖法

兩手摩腎堂三十六以數

多更妙

右法閉氣搓

手令熱後摩

腎堂如數畢

仍收手握固再閉氣想用心

火下燒丹田覺熱極即止

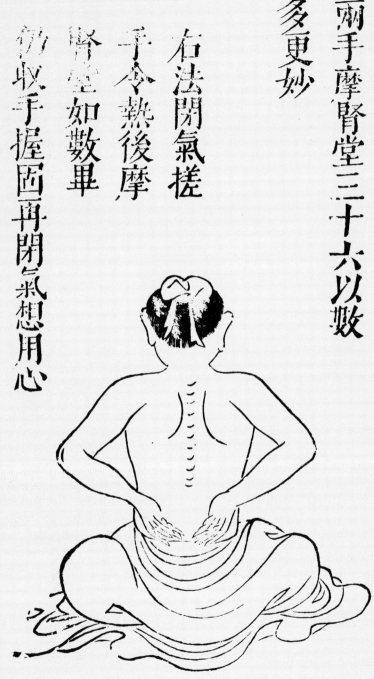

6: Therapeutic uses

Throughout this book we have pointed out that each of the soft arts has therapeutic properties, and that they not only keep you fit, but can actually be used to treat people who are suffering from illness or debilitating conditions. In Western medicine, exercise therapy is largely confined to physiotherapy, a specialist area that mainly helps with damaged muscles, ligaments, or bones. In China, though, exercise therapy is applied more broadly. The Chinese believe that illness is as often caused by an inappropriate lifestyle as by the attack of pathogenic agents. In the preceding chapter we examined how the Chinese encourage "balance" in their lives. Here we will look at how you can exercise to re-establish balance if it has been lost through ill health.

One of the basic problems with the Western approach to medicine is its tendency to treat the symptoms of an illness or imbalance and not to seek out the root causes. A secondary problem is over-reliance on drugs for therapy – often with inadequate regard for their toxic side-effects. Much of this chemical therapy is of very recent date, with tests and trials of relatively short duration. By contrast, Eastern medical systems are the product of thousands of years of experience, and their methods of treatment go to the origins of a disease, not to its simple manifestations.

Over the centuries, many different but complementary medical systems have evolved in the East – acupuncture and its partner acupressure, Chinese herbalism, and massage, for example. All of these systems adhere to the central aim of restoring and maintaining health with minimal resort to extreme interventions like strong drugs or surgery. About half of the health service of the People's Republic uses the traditional Chinese medical systems – and some of these therapies are now increasingly available in the Western world as well.

Exercise and training in the soft arts are an excellent means of preventing health problems, and they can provide a balanced treatment for illnesses too. In fact, in the course of their evolution, both Chi Kung and T'ai Chi Chuan have proved to be so beneficial that in some ways their therapeutic roles have superseded their martial uses. This chapter re-evaluates the arts described in Part One, and adds further remedies, including some from massage and acupressure. In general, the remedies advised here are intended to relieve two types of condition. First, they aim to resolve immediate problems like backache or headache. Second, they aim to help with chronic problems, such as anxiety or hypertension. However, if you suffer from such long-term problems, you should not expect instant results. Feeling the benefits of Chi Kung or T'ai Chi Chuan is a gradual process, and it may be weeks or even months before great changes take place. But when they do take place, you can be confident that they will be lasting, as long as you maintain your exercises.

Headaches

Chinese physicians recognize many different types of headaches – relating both to stress and fatigue and to heat or chilling, and involving many different organs and meridians. Most occasional headaches are a result of stress, tiredness, or overwork, and the best way to cope with them is to take preventive action – by avoiding the conditions that seem to cause them. Regular practice of any of the disciplines in Part One will help you to avoid and relieve such headaches – particularly the gentle arts of Chi Kung and T'ai Chi Chuan.

Headaches associated with constipation produce a full heavy pain in the forehead. Pain in the back of the head is often associated with the first signs of a cold. These pains are best relieved by practising the remedial exercises referred to in the tinted panel, right, and the acupressure and massage techniques described on the facing page. The general aim is to relax and ease the Chi flow through the meridians in the head, and to allow the Chi to flow downward, out of your "overfull" head.

If you suffer from migraine-type headaches, the first thing you should do is to check whether certain foods or drinks (coffee, chocolate, or red wine, for example) are acting as "triggers" for your headaches. This type of pain is often associated with Yang energy from the liver rising up in the body, and can be alleviated by doing exercises which develop Chi in your kidneys and liver. Smooth, rhythmic exercise forms such as the Ba Duan Jin, T'ai Chi, walking, or swimming, all help the uncontrolled hot energy to sink.

For headaches associated with the early stages of an infection like flu or a cold you should keep warm and make yourself sweat. Taking exercise is a good way to do this, as is having a hot bath. Alternatively, you can try a ginger footbath or just include more ginger in your diet. The source of many headaches lies in the digestive system. Problems there will often disrupt the flow of Chi to the head, and cause pain. It helps to ensure that your diet and eating habits are right for you (see A Balanced Diet, pp.154-61), and to practise the soft martial arts regularly, thus balancing the flow of Chi in the centre of your body.

In general, regular practice in the soft arts – whether Chi Kung (pp.22-43), Hsing I (pp.44-63), Pa Kua (pp.64-81), or T'ai Chi Chuan (pp.82-146) – will improve and protect your health. But some martial arts' exercises are indicated for particular conditions. The exercises listed in the tinted panels in this chapter serve this purpose. They should be practised in addition to the remedies described here.

Ba Duan Jin 5 for a hot, thumping headache p.31

Remedies for headaches

Apart from practising the soft arts, you can use both acupressure and massage to help relieve headaches. One very simple Eastern remedy is to gently massage the whole of your face with your fingers, using smooth downward strokes that stimulate the circulation of blood to the skin. (This is a well-known remedy, which comes from the Shier Duan Jin or the Twelve Fine Exercises.) Massaging the neck and shoulderblades helps too.

Acupressure on the brow

To relieve pain around the forehead, press firmly into the two slightly fleshy spots immediately above the ends of your eyebrows. Using the tips of your index and middle fingers, keep the pressure on for about 10 seconds, then relax it. Repeat until the headache eases.

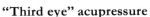

"Third eye" acupressure

Place the tip of your middle finger on the spot immediately above the ridge of your nose and slightly below the centre of your forehead. Press firmly for 10-20 seconds, then relax the pressure. Repeat until the pain recedes.

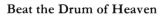

Beat the Drum of Heaven

This technique affects twin acupoints on either side of the cervical vertebrae. Place your hands on either side of your head with your fingers flat on the back of the neck. Drum your fingers at the base of the skull, for about a minute. The Chinese use this to relieve pain at the back of the head.

Hypertension

Problems of high blood pressure, or hypertension, and the less life-threatening problems of poor circulation and low blood pressure, are very common in the Western world. Doctors tend to tell their patients that their blood pressure is up or down, perhaps also giving them their blood pressure count, but few patients learn what this measurement really means. Being told that your blood pressure is above or below the average (which is usually defined as being around 120/80), doesn't tell you much.

What are these two mysterious figures anyway? The top reading represents the maximum pressure exerted when the heart squeezes to push the blood around the circulatory system. The lower figure is the pressure in the system at rest, at the moment when the pump of the heart is in between cycles.

Blood pressure varies from person to person, from minute to minute and day to day. All the organs in the body can contribute to imbalances which may result in the blood pressure being too high or low for the individual's well-being. It has even been confirmed recently that blood pressure readings taken by doctors tend to be higher than those taken by nurses, since many patients are nervous of doctors. (This is known as the "white coat hypertension" syndrome.) People who practise stamina sports often have lower blood pressure than average and many others live perfectly happily for years with blood pressure well above the norm. Healthy blood pressure should be whatever is appropriate for the individual, not a matter of conforming to the yardstick of normality.

For the Chinese, the key to understanding blood pressure is in the phrase "Blood is the mother of Chi, but Chi is the commander of blood". Blood is broadly understood as the substance that fills you up and gives you solidity, that makes your hair thick and your nails strong, that keeps your eyesight clear and gives you a sense of presence in the world. Blood in this sense is the ground from which vital energy springs. But it takes Chi to move it around the body. All the soft martial arts are dedicated to developing this balance of energy, so the best and most effective long-term way to ensure good flow of the blood and Chi in your body lies in regular practice of the exercises.

Gentle exercise, such as walking and swimming, is good, and massage is helpful. Any person with a serious heart condition should consult a physician about appropriate exercise.

Hsing I Pounding p.55
Ba Duan Jin, especially 5 for hypertension p.31
Ba Duan Jin 7 for low blood pressure p.33
Ba Duan Jin 8 for poor circulation p.33
Yang breathing p.25

Exercises for blood pressure problems

The Bellows Breathing shown below will improve your circulation and aid the heart, as will many other exercises which involve swinging the arms up and down or to each side. The Swinging Arms exercise shown on p.185 is another well-known example. These arm actions are very common in the warming-up exercises for the soft arts, and in the Ba Duan Jin.

Bellows Breathing

A *Imagine that your arms are a pair of bellows controlling your breathing. Stand upright and relaxed with your feet shoulders' width apart. Inhale as you raise both arms to shoulder height, with your elbows out to the sides and your hands to the front, palms facing forward and downward.*

A

B *Exhale through your nose as you lower your elbows to mid-chest height and bring your hands in toward the centre of your body, about 6 inches (15 cm) apart, still facing forward and downward. Repeat this action smoothly and slowly, at least 10 times.*

B

Anxiety, depression, and insomnia

The Chinese idea of anxiety and depression is very different from the Western one. Chinese physicians always consider that there is a clear cause for these states of mind, which may be treated internally, or by making some changes in the patient's environment. The problem may be located in a person's food, work, housing, or emotional life, and it is always possible to do something for the sufferer.

Traditional wisdom about the benefits of the soft arts for these kinds of problems has recently been endorsed by extensive clinical research in both China and the USA. In general it has been found that T'ai Chi Chuan is very helpful in the treatment of anxiety and depression, and for insomnia too – mainly due to the way it concentrates and calms the mind.

As Chinese physicians associate emotional states with specific organs in the body, emotional problems can be diagnosed and treated through the respective organs (p.151). Thus, for example, states of fear and paranoia relate to the kidneys; resentment, hopelessness, and frustration relate to the liver; feelings of lovelessness to the heart; worry and insecurity to the spleen; and a sense of loss or failure relates to the lungs. Practising the exercises which will work specifically on the appropriate organs will help people suffering from the emotional states connected with them. Treatment with other forms of Chinese medicine, such as acupuncture and herbalism, can also be highly successful.

Chi Kung (pp.22-43) and meditation (p.166) are calming for those suffering from anxiety, but they are less effective in depression. T'ai Chi helps all three conditions. Walking, jogging, and running also help to alleviate anxiety and insomnia.
Ba Duan Jin 2 and 5 p.28 and p.31
Ba Duan Jin 7, especially for debility p.33

Acupressure for insomnia
Sitting down on a firm chair or stool with both feet on the ground, place your left ankle on your right knee. Then, gripping the outside of the foot with your right hand, press your thumb firmly into the area just under the ball and toward the centre, as shown right. Maintain the pressure on this acupoint for about 10 seconds, then relax. Repeat on your right foot.

Digestive problems

Constipation, indigestion, obesity, and other problems related to digestion are now extremely common in the West, and an unsuitable lifestyle is probably the primary cause. The Chinese believe that simple inactivity often results in digestive troubles, so a first step for sufferers is to start regular exercise.

But, above all, digestive problems are caused by the type of foods we eat. Diets with over-high levels of proteins, fats, and acids, and low levels of fibre will always lead to digestive problems. Following the dietary guidelines given in Chapter 5 (pp.154-61) – as well as taking sensible exercise – will be very beneficial. Running, jumping, and jogging are recommended for people suffering from chronic constipation. Sit ups or rowing-type exercises and deep breathing (p.25) also help to strengthen the stomach wall, which in turn helps with constipation. Those with other long-term digestive problems should practise the Ba Duan Jin, Hsing I, and T'ai Chi, which are all good for the internal organs. Chi Kung is used to treat tension-related problems like indigestion and peptic ulcers.

Simple exercises that help to tone the digestive organs include circling legs (below), and exercises that involve squatting.

Ba Duan Jin 3 and 5 p.30 and p.31
Ba Duan Jin 6, especially in constipation p.32
Hsing I Crushing (Earth) p.52

Digestive massage
In a standing position as shown below, put your left hand on your Tan Tien (p.24), with your right hand on top of it. Press in gently then slowly circle your hands as shown right. This stimulates the digestive system.

Circling legs
Lie down on the floor with a cushion under your head. Raise both legs together, and gently roll them from side to side, 5 to 10 times. This is toning and stimulating.

Neck and back pain

The spinal column is quite literally what keeps the body upright. It is the core, and the protective housing for the central nervous system – but it is also a common source of bodily aches and pains.

There are many different reasons for neck ache and upper or lower back pain. Like headaches, they are sometimes caused by stress and fatigue, and the Chinese often relate them to problems in the internal organs such as the lungs, the kidneys, the gall bladder, or the liver. But the commonest cause of all is poor posture. A frequent fault in the West is to adopt a very rigid stance, pulling the shoulders backward and tucking the stomach in, a posture that actually creates backache and other spinal problems. A slouched position can be equally damaging. Poor posture is also exacerbated by badly designed seating at work and in cars and public transport – you may well end up stiff and sore after a long drive in the car, or simply after sitting at a desk all day. Regular practice in the soft arts will go a long way to correct your habits of posture, and to prevent serious problems developing. If you have persistent bad back pain, however, you should consult a medical specialist.

Swinging Arms and the Standing exercise for hips shown on p.185 are helpful for lower back problems.

Ba Duan Jin 2, especially for stiff shoulders p.28
Ba Duan Jin 6, but not if you have a problem with your lower back p.32

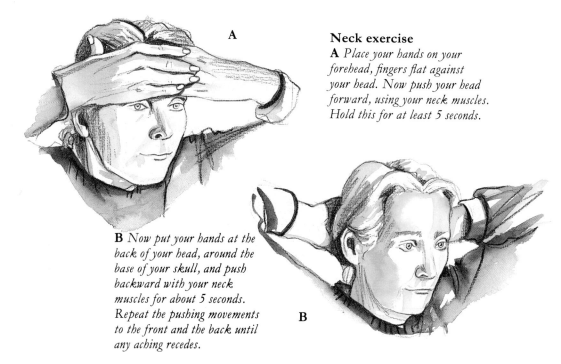

A

Neck exercise
A *Place your hands on your forehead, fingers flat against your head. Now push your head forward, using your neck muscles. Hold this for at least 5 seconds.*

B *Now put your hands at the back of your head, around the base of your skull, and push backward with your neck muscles for about 5 seconds. Repeat the pushing movements to the front and the back until any aching recedes.*

B

Neck massage

There is a series of acupoints which runs down each side of the top of the spine. Massage them with your fingertips to relieve tension in your neck, as shown on the right.

Lower back massage

To relieve pain in the mid to lower back area (around the kidneys), sit upright on a stool or hard chair, as shown below, and with your fingertips massage this area of your back on each side of your spine. If you feel you need a slightly deeper massage, turn your hands over and use your knuckles for the massage.

Back stretch

This is good for lower back troubles, and for stretching the legs. Sit on the floor with your legs straight out in front of you, as shown below. Lean forward and catch your toes with your hands, stretching your spine. Exhale as you go down, holding the stretch for 2-5 seconds, and inhale as you come back up again. If you are in pain, allow your knees to bend slightly. Repeat the stretch up to 10 times.

Rheumatism and arthritis

In traditional Chinese medicine, rheumatism and arthritis come under one category – the "blockage syndrome". The Chinese understanding of this range of afflictions is that at some point in your system the flow of blood and energy is blocked, like a river that has silted up. Such a blockage can develop from a number of sources – old injuries that never properly healed, over-use of a particular joint or limb, or an inappropriate diet leading to poisons polluting the flow in the body (like the gouty toe of a port drinker). Too hot, too cold, or damp living conditions, or a diet that is unsuitable for the individual – all these factors can lead to a jamming of the flow, with its painful consequences.

If you have a problem with associated back pain, the back exercises shown on p.181 and the one on the facing page should be useful. The lying-down exercise shown on p.185 may also help to relieve pain in the pelvis, and lower back. Ba Duan Jin 1 and 8 pp.26-7 and p.33 Ba Duan Jin 4, especially for stiffness or pain in the neck pp.30-1

The Chinese physician's prescription will depend on the answers to a number of questions. Does the rheumatism or arthritis get worse with cold weather? Then perhaps it would benefit from a hotter diet (pp.154-61). If things get worse in damp weather then it may well be that an accumulation of foods that produce dampness is part of the problem – that is, sugary foods and dairy products. Changing the diet to enhance the flow of blood and energy is often an important part of the healing process. As always with Chinese medicine there is no one answer for all conditions. Each person is an individual and the problems – and solutions – require that the physician looks at each person in the context of his or her own lifestyle.

Quite often, rheumatic or arthritic pains can be provoked by an isolated exposure to excessively cold or damp conditions. A good first-aid treatment for pain in the hands or feet is a footbath or handbath to which you add a large (golfball-sized) lump of fresh ginger that has been chopped up small. Ginger warms and moves the body's energy, and is very useful for clearing cold from your joints (p.160). If you feel that the cold has entered your bones you can even take a bath with a couple of pints of hot ginger infusion added to the water (make the infusion by steeping the chopped ginger in hot water for a few minutes). In general, anything that helps to get the Chi flowing will be helpful for rheumatism and arthritis. Gentle progressive exercise and massage can also be very beneficial.

Back and shoulder exercise

This exercise can provide relief for back and shoulder pain without risk of strain. Sit on a firm chair or stool, keeping your back upright, with your hands resting on your thighs. Then simply lean forward and slide your hands down your legs as far as you can go without strain. Return to the upright position, and repeat the exercise 5 times.

Cycling arms

For further relief from shoulder aches or stiffness, sit down on a firm chair or stool and move your arms rhythmically in a cycling action. Keep your fists lightly closed. Continue for 1 or 2 minutes, or until you tire.

Hands exercise

The Chinese use a pair of heavy metal balls called Baoding Tieqiu to exercise the hands. The balls are available through some martial arts' centres, and in some Chinese stores. They are pleasant to use – each one produces a gentle chiming note, one higher than the other (Yang as opposed to Yin). To exercise, make one ball move around the other in the palm of your hand for a minute or so. Then use the other hand.

Exercises for pregnancy

Pregnancy is not a debilitating condition, but it does place unique stresses and strains on the mother-to-be. Apart from the miraculous growth of the baby, some extremely acute changes take place within the mother's own body. In general it's fine to practise the gentle movements of the soft martial arts, but great care should be taken not to strain the joints and muscles. Chi Kung, and the gentle sequence of the Ba Duan Jin , may be practised throughout a normal pregnancy – though you may prefer to try the sitting exercises of Basic Chi Kung (p.36) as you get heavier. Hsing I and Pa Kua should be avoided, but T'ai Chi Chuan is fine for at least the first six months (after that some of the kicks and low sweeping movements should be omitted, until you are fully recovered from the birth).

Some of the ailments covered in this chapter tend to occur in the course of pregnancy. Any of the exercises and other remedies recommended will do you good, since they are gentle and harmless, but you should always take care. Check with a doctor if you are in any doubt at all.

Ba Duan Jin 1 and 3 pp.26-7 and p.30

One of the more extraordinary effects of pregnancy is the release of a hormone that allows every joint in the body to open up and become loose. As the baby grows, this stimulates the chest cavity to expand by up to 3 inches (5 cm), so that some of the internal organs can move up above the expanding womb. However, the same hormone also allows the spinal joints to expand, and this is a common cause of lower back pain and aches in other areas, especially as the baby gets heavier to carry. It is especially important not to try to relieve backache by practising any exercise that requires you to lie down on your back and then lift your hips off the ground. These movements only place added strain on your joints. Instead, you should try the lower back massage shown on page 181, and the toning movements shown on the facing page. It is also essential that you take due care of your back after the birth, since your body will still be vulnerable to strain. This is a time when it pays to take regular gentle exercise if you can, maintain good posture (p.180), and to avoid unnecessary strain – such as the damage caused by bending-over-and-lifting movements. You should bend at the knees and take the weight on your arms if you are lifting anything from below waist height (see also p.170).

Some exercises for pregnant women aim to promote general fitness, some to prepare the woman for the birth itself, but all gentle exercise is of great benefit.

Standing exercise for hips

Stand with your feet shoulders' width apart, and put your hands on the back of your hips, palms inward. Shift your weight sideways onto your right leg, then shift back to the centre and onto your left leg. Continue to sway slowly from side to side.

Swinging Arms

This is an excellent gentle exercise to strengthen the body, increase energy, and improve circulation. It is very popular in China. Simply stand upright with your feet shoulders' width apart and your arms by your sides. Turn your hands so that the palms face forward, and swing your arms together, forward and up to shoulder height, then down and to the back. The number of times you repeat this depends on your condition – 200 times is a normal daily prescription for a healthy person.

Lying-down exercise

This helps to prepare you for childbirth. Lie down on your back with a thin cushion under your head and shoulders and your arms flat by your sides. Raise both your knees, keeping your feet flat on the floor, then allow them to fall open as far as they will go without straining. Hold this position for 2-5 seconds, then bring your knees together. Repeat 20 times.

Exercises for the elderly

In the West it is commonly assumed that as the body gradually ages it becomes more frail, and increasingly beset with physical problems. It is true that the body does tend to stiffen up, and begins to respond less well to standard medical treatments. According to Chinese tradition, the vital energy stored in the kidneys starts to decline, and circulates less freely through the body.

This is where the soft arts come into their own, gently revitalizing the body. Clinical tests carried out in China have established that older people who practise T'ai Chi or Chi Kung are in appreciably better health than those of the same age who do not do so, especially in terms of stronger hearts and better respiration and circulation, as well as general flexibility. If you suffer from a chronic illness you should always seek medical advice before taking up a martial art for the first time. And when you start your practice it may be some months before you begin to feel the benefits. But when changes do take place they will greatly improve your health.

Swinging Arms, described on p.185, is a good alternative to Swinging Hands, facing page.
Ba Duan Jin 1-8 pp.26-33

Knee and spine exercise
A *Stand with your feet shoulders' width apart, and inhale as you raise your arms to the sides.*

B *Exhale as you bend your knees and swing both arms down, crossing the wrists. Then inhale as you raise your arms to shoulder height again, and straighten your legs. Repeat the swing 5 times.*

Swinging Hands

Standing with your feet about shoulders' width apart, turn your torso as you gently swing your arms to the left. Look to the left at the same time. Now let your arms swing like a pendulum – swing back to the right, then to the left, and so on, at least 5 times to each side.

Dragon Stamping

From the standing position shown on the facing page, go slowly right up onto your tiptoes, as high as you can. Stretch your body upward. At the same time point your fingers down and inward, stretching your arms downward. Return your heels to the ground and relax. Repeat 5 times.

Strengthening leg point

Pressing this acupressure point is good for general health, and for digestive problems. The point lies at the top of the shin bone, in the curve where the bone widens toward the knee. To find it, run your thumb up the outside of the bone until you feel the curve. Then press quite deeply 20 times.

Asthma

Asthma may be difficult to treat, since it can develop from several sources and be perpetuated by a number of different things. There may also be a hereditary tendency, but the Chinese believe that asthma can be alleviated, if not cured, in all but a few cases. Asthma is always related to problems with the respiratory system, and any exercise for the lungs is helpful, such as the breathing exercises described in Chapter 5 (pp.167-9), Ba Duan Jin 1-4 (pp.26-31), and Hsing I Splitting (pp.50-1). Other vital organs, however, may be involved too.

Anyone with asthma should avoid all foods which promote mucus production, notably dairy products. Mucus is a major component in asthma – it can make its presence felt as hard tightness in the chest, or it can provoke coughing and deep wheezing. According to Chinese medicine, it is produced by the spleen and stomach. If these organs are overwhelmed with certain kinds of fatty food they can't deal with, or they are under pressure from a lot of heat from the liver, or smoking or an infection, for example, then they will produce excess mucus. The Chinese also believe that too much thinking provokes over-production of mucus, so there is a need to balance your intellectual activity with physical activity and meditation. Try massaging tight or tense areas of the chest with outward and downward strokes. Western drugs, helpful though they may be, tend in the long term to have a debilitating effect both physically – affecting the lungs, kidneys, and liver – and mentally, since they often bring the sufferer into a state of dependency which hampers his or her recovery. You may find that you feel worse when you are stressed, angry, or tired. In each case, the soft arts will help, enabling you to be more strong and flexible in the face of stress, or to find the inner resources to cope with your anger. You may just need to rest a lot to recharge your batteries – especially if you get wheezy every evening after a day's work. Another factor, often over-looked in the West but considered important in Chinese medicine, is the influence of the intestines (the sister of the lungs) on your breathing. For many people, constipation will bring on an attack of asthma. So a suitable diet and exercise may well be helpful.

Index

Numbers in **bold** refer to major entries

Acupressure, 152, 173
  for digestion, 187
  for headaches, 175
  for insomnia, 178
acupuncture, 152, 173
anger, *see* emotions
anxiety, 83, **178**
Apparent Close Up, 137
arthritis, **182-3**
asthma, 158, **188**

Back exercises, 87, **180-1,** 183
back strain, avoiding, 170-1, 184
Ba Duan Jin, 17, **26-33**
Basic Chi Kung, **34-6**
Basic Powers (or Forces), **140-3**
Beat the Drum of Heaven, 175
Bellows Breathing, 177
bladder, and Five Elements, 151,
  153
"blockage syndrome", 182
blood, 176
  foods for, 157, 160
blood pressure, 176
  See also high and low blood
  pressure
Bodhidharma, 14
Book of Changes, *see* I Ching
breathing, 24, **25,** 150, **166-9**
  exercises, 25, 165, 167-9
Brush Knee and Twist Hip, 97-9
Buddhism, 12, 13, 14

Chi, 23, **24,** 149, **150-3**
  and sexual balance, 164
  strengthening foods, 157
childbirth, exercise for, 185
Chi Kung, 16, 17, **22-43**
  Basic Chi Kung, 34-6
  Chi Kung walk, 42-3
  Intermediate Chi Kung, 37-41
circulatory system, 83, 176-7
Closing Form, 139
colds, foods for, 155, 157, 160
colic, foods to avoid, 158, 160
Commencing Form, 47-9
Conception Vessel, 165
Confucianism, 12, 13
conjunctivitis, 157, 160
constipation, 179, 188

convalescents' diet, 157, 158
Cool Excess Heat, 31
cosmology, 150
coughs, foods for, 157, 158
Cow Looks at the Moon Behind,
  30-1
Cross Hands, 138
Cycle of Control, **153**
Cycle of Creation, **153**

Dairy products, 157
Daoyin, 16
defence, *see* self defence
depression, 160, **178**
diarrhoea, foods for, 156, 158, 160
diet, **154-61**
digestive problems, 107, 179
Dragon, 62
Dragon Embracing Moon, 119
Dragon Stamping, 187

Eagle, 62
Earth, 151, 152, 153
  Earth foods, 154
  emotions, 162
  exercise, 56
  See also Five Elements
eight diagrams 64, 66
Eight Fine Exercises, *see* Ba
  Duan Jin
Eight Fixed Postures **72-5**
elderly, exercises for **186-7**
emotions, **162**
  and Five Elements, 151, 162
"empty step" (T'ai Chi), 96
energy, vital, *see* Chi

Fear, *see* emotions
Fire, 151, 153
  emotions, 162
  exercise, 5
  See also Five Elements
Five Elements, 46, 151, 152, 153
  exercises, 48-59
  and foods, 154
food, preparation of, 161
  See also diet
"Four Corners", 90, 127
four directions, of foods, 154
four natures, of foods, 154

Gall bladder, and Five Elements,
  151, 153
gastro-intestinal disorders, 107

ginger, baths, 155, 160, 174,
  182-3
Governing Vessel, 165
Grasp the Bird's Tail,
  Left/Right, 104-6, 107-9
grief, *see* emotions

Hand Strums Lute, 100
hands exercise, 183
headaches, 155, **174-5**
heart
  exercises for, 55, 169, 177
  and Five Elements, 151, 153
Heaven and Earth, 91
herbalism, Chinese, 160, 173
high blood pressure, 83, 176
hips exercise, 185
"hold ball" gesture, 92
Hsing I, 16, **44-63**
  Five Elements exercises, 46-59
  Twelve Animals, 60-3
hypertension, 160, **176-7**

"I", 44, 46
I Ching, 13, 64, 66
impotence, *see* sexual balance
Increase the Chi, 33
indigestion, 156, 179
insomnia, 83, 156, **178**
Intermediate Chi Kung, **37-41**

Jing, 164

Kick with Right Heel, 117-8
kidneys
  exercises for, 32, 169
  and Five Elements, 151, 153
  foods for, 156, 157, 158, 160
knee exercises, 86, 186
Kung Fu, sexual, 164

Lao Tzu, 12, 14, 24
leg exercises, 87
lifestyle, 18-9, 149, 171
liver,
  exercise for, 52
  and Five Elements, 151, 153
  foods for, 156, 157, 158
longevity, 96, 164
low blood pressure, 176
lumbago, 156, 158
lungs,
  exercises for, 50, 169
  and Five Elements, 151, 153
  foods for, 158, 160

Massage therapy, 173
    digestive, 179
    lower back, and neck, 181
medicinal foods, 156-61
medicine
    Chinese, 151, 154, 173
meditation, 9, 18, 83, **166**
meridians, 151, **152**, 165
Metal, 151, 153
    emotions 162
    exercise, 50
    See also Five Elements
migraine, 156, 174
Monkey, 63
mucus, excess, 156, 157, 158
    and asthma, 188

Nature, 46, 149
neck pain, 180-1
Nei Ching, 23

Obesity, 179
Old Lady Works the Shuttles to
    Both Sides, 127-30
organs, internal, 152
    exercises for, 26-33, 48-59, 169
    and Five Elements, 151, 152

Pa Kua, 16, 17, **64-81**
    Eight Fixed Postures, 72-5
    Pa Kua walking, 67-71
    Palm Changes, 76-81
paranoia, 178
Part the Wild Horse's Mane to
    Both Sides, 92-5
peptic ulcers, 179
physiotherapy, 173
"Playing the Pipa", 100
Pluck the Needle from the Sea
    Bottom, 131
posture, 25, 170, 180
pregnancy, exercises, **184-5**
psychological states, debilitating, 83
"Push Down and Stand on One
    Leg", 123-4
Pushing Hands, **144-6**

Qi, *see* Chi

Regulate the Internal Organs, 26
Regulate Spleen and Stomach, 30
Repulse the Monkey, 101-2
respiratory system, 83, 188
rheumatism, 156, 182-3
Roll Back, 141
rootedness, 84-5

San Ti, *see* Three Essentials
self defence, 10, 84-5, **140-6**

self-knowledge, 9, 170-1
"Separating the Hands", 132
sexual balance, **164-5**
    foods for, 156, 158, 160
Shier Duan Jin, 175
Shoot the Eagle, 28-9
Short Form (T'ai Chi), 83, **90-139**
shoulder exercise, 86, 183
Shoulder Strike, 140
Single Whip (1 and 2), 110-1, 115
Six Sounds, 169
Snake Creeps Down, Left/Right,
    123-4, 125-6
sore throats, foods for, 157, 160
spiritual training, 83, 149, 166
spleen
    exercises for, 30, 169
    and Five Elements, 151, 152
stomach
    exercise for, 30
    and Five Elements, 151, 152
    foods for, 154, 156, 157
Strengthen the Kidneys, 32
Stretching the Heel, 117-8
"Strike Opponent's Ears with
    Both Fists", 119
Supreme Pole Boxing, 83
Swallow, 62
Swinging Arms, 177, 185
Swinging Hands, 187
sympathy, *see* emotions
T'ai Chi Chuan, 10, 16, 17,
    82-146
    Basic Powers, 140-3
    Pushing Hands, 144-5
    Short Form, 90-139
    T'ai Chi walk, 88-9
Ta Mo, 14
Tan Tien, **24**
Tao, *see* the Way
Taoism, 12, 44, 46
    breathing exercises, 91, 167-9
Tao Te Ching, 13, 25, 84, 171
Three Essentials, 47
Tiger, 60-1
Tiger's mouth position, 47, 48
time, and Five Elements, 151
Twelve Animals, 60-3
Twelve Fine Exercises, *see* Shier
    Duan Jin
Twin Dragon Searches for the
    Pearl, 119
Turn, Deflect, Parry, and Punch,
    133-6
Turn and Kick with Left Heel,
    120-2

Walking, 170
    Chi Kung walk, 42-3
    Pa Kua walk, 67-71
    T'ai Chi walk, 88-9
Ward Off Illness by Shaking the
    Body, 33
Water, 151, 153
    emotions, 162
    exercise, 54
    See also Five Elements
Wave Hands Like Clouds, 112-5
Way, the (Tao), 12, 20, 24, 149,
    171
White Crane Spreads Wings, 96
Wood, 151, 153
    emotions, 162
    exercise, 52
    See also Five Elements
Wu Te ("martial virtues"), 14

Yellow Emperor's Classic of
    Internal Medicine, 23
yielding, 84-5
Yin and Yang, 24, 84, 150, 164
    breathing, 169
    foods, 154
    people, 150
Yoga, 150

Zen buddhism, 14

Bibliography
Chee Soo, *Taoist Yoga*, Aquarian Press, London, 1983

Dahong Zhuo, *The Chinese Exercise Book*, Thorsons Publishing Wellingborough / New York, 1984

Da Liu, *The Tao of Health and Longevity*, Routlege Kegan and Paul, London, 1978

Lao Tzu, *Tao Te Ching* (trans. Ch'u Ta-Kao), George Allen & Unwin Ltd, London, 1937

Lu, Henry C., *Chinese System of Food Cures*, Blandford Press

Mantak, Chia and Winn, Michael, *Taoist secrets of love*, Aurora Press, New York, 1984

Reid, Howard and Croucher, Michael, *The Way of the Warrior*, Century Hutchinson Ltd, London, 1986

Smith, Robert W., *Pa-Kua*, Kodansha International, 1967

Smith, Robert W., *Hsing-I*, Kodansha International, 1974

Author's acknowledgments
Many people have contributed to the preparation of this book by giving me their time and by allowing me to use time which I should have spent with them to work on this book. First and foremost this applies to my wife and to my two children Amie and Leila. It applies too to my mother Pat, brother Simon, and two sisters Jan and Fiona.

I owe special debt to the chief consultants for Part One – Lam Kam Chuen, Danny Connor, and Nigel Sutton – and to Robin Rusher who provided much excellent material for Part Two. All of the contributors to the book have given freely of their time and thought and I would like to thank them all, and to specially thank Riete Oord for her patience.

All at Gaia Books have been highly supportive, Phil Wilkinson, who started editing the book, Ros Mair, who finished it, Sara Mathews for fine art direction, and Lucy Lidell for skilful management of the work. Finally may I acknowledge my deep debt to Dr. Peter Silverwood-Cope and to Master Hung I-Hsiang who introduced me to the martial arts and the internal arts respectively.

Gaia's acknowledgments
Gaia would like to thank all those in Trundle Street who gave generously of their help – especially Lesley Gilbert, Helen Banbury, and Eve Webster. We are also grateful to Danny Connor, Lam Kam Chuen, and Nigel Sutton, for their patience and generosity in guiding the martial arts' photography for this book. The following models contributed their time and expertise: Leon Bryce, John Spencer Gardiner, Ayumu Kawajiri, Lai Chan, Caroline Lissant, Mew Hong Tan, Erik Ness, Ruth O'Dowd, Fons Sarneel, Odette Slater, Alice Stopozynski, Jill Sugden, David Watson, and Marek Ziebart. Debbie Hinks is owed a special thankyou for her contribution to illustration; and Brian McKenzie and Mew Hong Tan also lent artistic assistance. Beth McKillop, Oriental Department of the British Library, gave expert help in choosing oriental images. Assistance with translation and Pin Yin came from Howard Reid's assistant Yin King Chiu.

Quotations from Lao Tzu's *Tao Te Ching* (trans. Ch'u Ta-Kao), George Allen & Unwin Ltd, London, 1937, appear on pages 6, 25, 84, and 171, by kind permission of Unwin Hyman Ltd, London/Sydney.

The following associations and instructors are recommended by the consultants for this book: Danny Connor, Qi Gong Institute, 18 Swan Street, Manchester M4 5JN; Lam Kam Chuen (of the Lam T'ai Chi and Da Cheng Chuan Chi Kung Associations), c/o Y.W.C.A. Central Club, 16-22 Great Russell St, London WC1B 3LR, and 79 Princess Avenue, London W3 8LX; Nigel Sutton, Zhijiang Taijiquan Yanjiu Xueyuan, Ealing College Upper School, 83 The Avenue, London W13 8JS; Julian Abel (UK contact for Bruce Frantzis, Santa Fe, USA), Wu-style T'ai Chi, Chatley Barn, Linch Lane, Batcombe, Somerset; Paul Crompton, T'ai Chi Chuan, Lily Road Fitness Centre, London SW6; Dan Docherty, Wutan T'ai Chi Chuan, 45 Aston House, Wandsworth Rd, London SW8 4ER; D.R.Frearson, British T'ai Chi Chuan and Shaolin Kung Fu Association, 28 Linden Farm Drive, Countesthorpe, Leics LE8 3SX; R.C.Wilkie, Yi Chuan Chang School of Internal Martial Arts, 23 Oakwood Ave, Mitcham, Surrey CR4 3DQ; Simon Wong, Yellow Dragon Combined T'ai Chi Mantis, 341 Prince Regent Lane, Custom House, London E16; Gary Wragg, Wu-style T'ai Chi Chuan, Regents Park Martial Arts & Health Club, Albany St, London NW1; The Martial Arts Commission, 1st Floor, Broadway House, 15/16 Deptford Broadway, London SE8 4PE.

Photographic credits
All of the photographs in this book were taken by Fausto Dorelli, with the following exceptions: p.6 The Image Bank, St Martins Lane, London WC2; p.11 Rodney Wilson; p.15, 148, 172, and endpapers – by permission of the British Library; p.159 Greg Evans Photolibrary, Charlotte St, London W1.

Typesetting
Hourds Typographica, Stafford, England

Reproduction
David Bruce Graphics, London.